Praise for *Excellence at Work* and Author Sandy Asch

"In the Information Systems department at Mitchell International, we have used the Excellence principles to keep employees focused on priorities and establish a positive work environment. Turnover is at an unprecedented low of 4%."
—**Linda Amaro**, Vice President, Information Systems, Mitchell International

"Sandy's 'Excellent Workplace Model' provides a viable roadmap and an excellent jumpstart to create a work environment in which every employee has a sense of pride, loyalty and belonging."
—**Jack Giles**, CEO, REMEC Defense and Space, Inc.

"Sandy Asch is passionately dedicated to creating uncommonly inspiring paths for individuals, teams and organizations to achieve excellence in ways they cannot imagine. She begins by exhibiting highly professional standards in her training workshops, and now in her book, *Excellence at Work*, Sandy offers a unique 'excellence code' based on six Excellence principles, which, when deeply embraced by an organization can transform its culture. The six principles optimize employees' day-to-day work experiences, levels of engagement, interpersonal and team functioning, and ultimately organizational performance. This is one business book to study carefully and implement immediately."
—**Judith L. Enns, Ph.D.**, Executive Vice President, HR Solutions

"I am thrilled that Sandy Asch has published *Excellence at Work*. Sandy uses integrity, intelligence and humor to demonstrate standards of behavior and offers useful takeaways in her book. She delivers insightful manager tools to employers for the success of their company's vision and focused best practices. Sandy brings *passion* to the workplace."
—**Wendy Evers**, Senior Director of Program Development, San Diego State University
President, North County Personnel Association

"Finally! I have worked on synchronizing and monitoring the success of strategic planning and budgeting processes in companies of all sizes. For two decades metrics from human capital management have been conspicuous by their absence. With this book Sandy has provided a framework for business intelligence dashboards to include the pulse of that most crucial element of any corporate initiative: the people."
—**David Moore**, President, Business Avionics, LLC

"Sandy utilizes a revolutionary approach to attract, engage, optimize and retain top-tier talent. I strongly recommend that all HR practitioners incorporate these proven strategies into their organizations to distinguish themselves from their competitors."
—**Michael Milligan**, Human Resources & General Affairs Manager,
Toppan Optical Products, Inc.

"As a CFO, my goal is to create value in the organization. The Excellence program helps to build an environment where people can be most effective, become as good as they are, and even better than they should be, thereby adding value. The program has served to decrease the 'human friction' and establish an environment of creativity, innovation, trust and respect—all essential elements of a successful company. Modern Postcard's continued growth and increased profitability is proof we have achieved 'excellence.' Some might ask how we can afford to offer a program like this to our entire employee population. I ask, 'How can we afford not to?'"

—**Bill Lofft**, Former CFO, Modern Postcard

"Sandy provides a systematic model to build a sustainable 'employer-of-choice' organization."
—**Marc Brown**, Vice President, Human Resources, Encore Capital Group Inc.

"The Excellence program opened a lot of eyes and challenged many assumptions about what is possible in a government agency. While each participant was positively affected in unique ways, the entire leadership was re-energized with a new commitment to changing the culture of the agency to one that brings out the very best in every staff member. The program systematically laid out the Excellence principles and promoted the kinds of practices that we've always wanted but didn't know how to achieve."
—**Tom Cullen**, Former CFO, Catawba Community Mental Health Center, Rock Hill, SC

"In today's marketplace, attracting and keeping top talent is critical to having a successful and thriving business. The Excellence principles create a culture of high standards and high results, which fully engage every member of your staff. Such a culture not only retains top talent, but helps you to become an employer-of-choice where top talent is waiting in line to get on board."
—**Edi Holderman**, Human Resources Manager, Vistage International, Inc.

"I participated in the Excellence program with Sandy seven years ago and it was life changing. Working in the government sector, I initially felt our environment was not conducive to these ideas. However, Sandy helped inspire my journey to a new way of leadership beyond my visible boundaries and I have never looked back!"
—**Rob Claudio**, Member, Board of Directors,
International Association of Workforce Professionals

"There are many new business programs designed to 'fix' your organization that are no more than a fad. Sandy's use of visuals, statistics and stories has a long-lasting impact on an organization as compared to other programs I have utilized in the past. The Excellence program really helps an organization re-energize their people and 'make it happen.' Thanks for the inspiring information. These are great tools."
—**Wendy Crawford**, Director, Human Resources, Salinas Valley Memorial Hospital

EXCELLENCE
• *at* •
WORK

The Six Keys to Inspire Passion in the Workplace

Sandy Asch

About WorldatWork®

WorldatWork (www.worldatwork.org) is the association for human resources professionals focused on attracting, motivating and retaining employees. Founded in 1955, WorldatWork provides practitioners with knowledge leadership to effectively implement total rewards—compensation, benefits, work-life, performance and recognition, development and career opportunities—by connecting employee engagement to business performance. WorldatWork supports its 30,000 members and customers in 30 countries with thought leadership, education, publications, research and certification.

The WorldatWork group of registered marks includes: WorldatWork®, workspan®, Certified Compensation Professional or CCP®, Certified Benefits Professional® or CBP, Global Remuneration Professional or GRP®, Work-Life Certified Professional or WLCP™, WorldatWork Society of Certified Professionals®, and Alliance for Work-Life Progress® or AWLP®.

WorldatWork.
The Total Rewards Association
www.worldatwork.org

©2007 Sandy Asch
ISBN 978-157963-169-7 (Paperback/softback)
   978-1-57963-238-0 (E-book)

Acknowledgments

Thank you to the thousands of participants in my Excellence programs. When your eyes sparkled, I was reminded how valuable these simple truths are.

I would also like to thank Pat MacEnulty for her faith in this book and the generosity of spirit she brought to this project; Tom Cullen for being an astute matchmaker; Pattie Vargas, Lee Sharp, Bob Scheid, John J. Cotter, Marian Donahue, Judy Enns and Wendy Crawford for believing; Linda Brawley-Carol for beginning the Excellence journey with me; David Moore for his grand vision and unquestionable support; and Sarai Rodgers for her "shining eyes" and always saying "yes."

Special thanks to the publishing team at WorldatWork for your dedication to this project, and in particular, my gratitude to Dan Cafaro for expanding the WorldatWork portfolio to include *Excellence at Work*. Your honesty and commitment to our partnership has made this adventure a delight.

To Soudabeh Memarzad, Kyle Amdahl, Jason Brousseau and the creative team at Modern Postcard, I thank you for your brilliance.

This book is dedicated to my son, Adam Lee Sloane. The grace, ease and joy with which you live your life is an inspiration. I am blessed by your presence in my life.

Table of Contents

"Excellence is an art won by training and habituation. We do not act rightly because we have virtue or excellence, but we rather have those because we have acted rightly. We are what we repeatedly do. Excellence, then, is not an act but a habit."

—Will Durant (commonly attributed to Aristotle)

Dear Priyanka:
Be courageous.
Be bold. Be powerful!
Best wishes,
Sandy

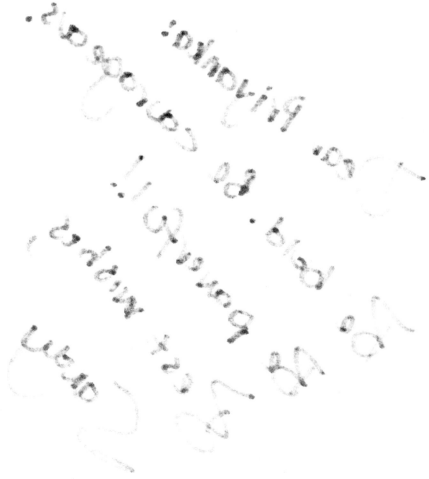

Preface

My passion is to make the workplace exciting and joyful—a place where people experience pride, satisfaction and fulfillment. I believe this is only possible in an environment in which employees feel passionate about their work. This is, I know, a revolutionary idea. We don't generally equate passion and work. Work is thought to be a series of necessary tasks, at best, and drudgery, at worst. But if the leaders of an organization establish a culture of excellence through their personal attitudes, behaviors and expectations, they can inspire passion in their employees and create a dynamic work environment.

My method of achieving passion through excellence is based on the idea that each individual is responsible for creating a healthy, fulfilling work environment— a place in which work can be play, and play can be profitable. This approach is also built on the belief that by making a personal commitment to excellence, you can improve all aspects of your life and positively influence those around you.

When I began presenting the Excellence program for businesses, it was a small part of a traditional tactical leadership program. But it was the part that audiences responded to best—and the part they repeatedly asked me to expand. The program evolved over the next 10 years as a result of training presentations to thousands of leaders in more than 250 companies and my personal commitment to ongoing personal and professional excellence.

This evolutionary process produced the Six Excellence Principles described in this book, and the tools that are provided to implement them. Why do I believe so deeply in these "Excellence principles"? In addition to witnessing their effectiveness in a variety of workplaces, I use them as my own compass in all my personal and professional dealings. These six principles (or keys) of excellence have become a part of everything I do. When I began to consistently use them in my own life and work, I noticed immediate results. The effect was life-altering and life-enhancing.

Even though I could see the powerful effects of living and working by the Excellence principles, at first I presented them with trepidation, wondering if audiences would "get it," or if they would think the principles were too "touchy-feely."

To my surprise and delight, I found that, regardless of their position in their organization, job responsibilities, industry, age or gender, participants responded with enthusiasm. From executive leaders in high-tech companies to frontline community service providers to high school students, participants have grasped the value and relevance of these principles.

I owe my success in large part to these principles. I live them and breathe them. Even though I do not always perfectly follow them, I am committed to them. People know I stand for excellence. That's a great thing to be known for. When you role model excellence, people remember you and are inspired to hold themselves to a higher standard, too.

I have been astonished at the number of people I have encountered who, years after learning the Excellence principles, still remember every one of the principles and delight in reciting them to me, describing how they still use the principles to maintain a high level of focus and morale. An engineer who participated in the Excellence program at least five years earlier recently called to me from across the grocery store parking lot to tell me he still remembers to avoid downward spiral conversations (Chapter 5) and to speak possibility. He went on to explain that his department has managed to stay positive despite an overwhelming workload and persistent organizational change. This interaction was especially amusing since he couldn't remember my name, and resorted to calling me the "excellence lady."

Over the years, I have come to realize that the Excellence principles are an essential foundation for organizational success. They are the "glue" that makes human resources, training initiatives and business processes "stick" and produce lasting results. What good does it do to invest resources in training employees on new customer service skills or to implement a new quality program if your employees don't have a foundational commitment to excellence?

Numerous clients have requested a comprehensive guide to help them integrate the Excellence principles in their organization. They realized, as have I, that no matter how valuable their individual use of the principles is, in order for the program to have lasting effect, they needed a way to achieve sustainable organizational change. Excellence at Work is the answer to their requests. Through this book, I offer you these principles, examples of their effectiveness, and tools and strategies for operationalizing them in your workplace. I believe they will make a difference—not just in your work life but in your personal life, as well.

Wishing you continued success!

—*Sandy Asch*

Introduction

A group of senior executives from a successful manufacturing company was intrigued by a simple question I posed in an executive off-site meeting: "Where is the Excellence Thermostat set in your company?" After much consideration, the group agreed that, on average, the level of employee excellence was about 60 percent to 70 percent. When asked if they were satisfied with their assessment, the executives responded with a resounding "no!" They had realized, as have leaders in many companies, that if employees are falling short of their potential, lack passion and engage in unproductive behaviors that deplete their time, energy and focus, the company will be challenged to meet its goals. It was clear that if their company was going to meet its aggressive revenue goals and be recognized as a leader in the industry, every employee would have to contribute at his or her highest level.

The Excellence Thermostat is a straightforward tool for identifying the standards of behavior to which employees are held. In many companies, such standards have eroded over time and resulted in organizationwide acceptance of gossip, criticism, complaint and condemnation. These behaviors in turn caused victim behaviors, "road kill" and general disengagement. In the case of the manufacturing client, an Excellent Workplace survey by Alliance for Organizational Excellence LLC showed that only 35 percent of employees were fully engaged—energized and motivated—by their work. For the remaining 65 percent of employees who admitted they were frustrated, resigned, barely interested in their work or just "coasting," the following question arises: "What must the leadership do to reinvigorate and refocus employees on success?"

Most companies face overwhelming pressure to produce more, better, faster and cheaper in order to compete in a demanding global marketplace. To this we can add a shrinking workforce, an all-time low unemployment rate for college graduates and a projected labor shortfall of 26 million skilled workers. Leaders will thus be increasingly challenged to extract the greatest value from a multiethnic, four-generation workforce, each generation of which has unique needs and demands. Failure to meet this challenge will put many companies at risk.

To be an "Excellent Organization" requires a new mind-set, a new set of habits and a whole new design of a company's corporate culture. The new culture must be one in which there is a passionate commitment to excellence that is characterized by high productivity, full engagement and inspired leadership. Establishment of this culture enables companies to attract, optimize and retain the top talent they need in order to meet and exceed their business goals. *Excellence at Work* provides a practical road map for leaders at every level in an organization to do just that.

Research findings that suggest that establishing a strong corporate culture will help your business gain competitive advantage have been available for 30 years. So why haven't most companies already done it? The answer is that few people welcome change, and most can't make the leap from concept to action, which is why we spell it out in *Excellence at Work*. As you follow the steps I provide, you will establish a new set of standards or expectations for the way in which your people go about their day-to-day responsibilities. The goal is to lock in the Excellence principles so they become pervasive and embedded in every aspect of your business.

In companies where the Excellence principles have become "the way" and are accepted as the standard, the results have been remarkable. Excellence graduates report that the use of these principles has had a profound and lasting effect on them, as follows:

- 75 percent report they increased productivity by 10 percent to 50 percent.
- 95 percent communicate more effectively.
- 87 percent are more accountable.
- 91 percent improved relationships with internal and external customers.
- 89 percent bring more energy and passion to work every day.
- 76 percent are more effective leaders.

The effect of the Excellence principles on an organization goes far beyond these statistics and positively influences every aspect of organizational life. In one case, a vice president and a senior director who had barely spoken to one another for three years, other than to exchange insults and engage in screaming matches within the earshot of employees, called a truce. The two have since transformed their relationship and now conduct themselves in a professional and even colle-gial manner. By making this new "agreement" to treat each other with respect and dignity, they communicated to employees that it was no longer acceptable to behave unprofessionally. After all, what we allow, we teach.

Although individual successes have been significant, the greatest successes have come from organizationwide application of the principles. Where senior leadership has committed to integrating the Excellence principles and incorporating the Excellence Code, and has invested the time and resources to include all employees in the process, the results have been significant.

The San Diego Workforce Partnership's forward-thinking leadership team, after participating in the Excellence training itself, decided unanimously to implement the Excellence principles enterprisewide. The Excellence principles quickly became the new shared language and served as a powerful compass for daily actions and behaviors at a time when employees were faced with a great deal of uncertainty due to budget cuts, reorganization and layoffs.

Employees at another company were so inspired that they created a game based on the principles. We will discuss this game later in the book and show you how to create an Excellence Game for your workplace, and we will provide other tools that will help you implement the principles. I believe deeply in the power of play and joy to create and sustain excellence at work. You can experience similar successes in your company by following the guidelines and implementing the strategies outlined in this book.

W. Edwards Deming said that the ultimate business of business is the human spirit. That is, business should provide people with the opportunity to flourish and thrive. We cannot measure "spirit," but we can always tell when it is lacking in an organization. A workplace in which employees are tense and fear-ridden cannot foster creativity and sustain high performance. However, an environment that honors and respects the human spirit of all workers can only be a success. Committed leaders can create that environment. *Excellence at Work* offers them the blueprint.

The first part of the book, "Getting in the Game," answers the question: "Why do you need the Excellence principles?" Its four chapters offer a rationale for implementing an excellence initiative, demonstrate the costs of employee disengagement and offer an overview of the Excellence principles. Part Two of the book, "The Principles, or The Rules of the Game," explains each principle in depth and provides examples of desirable behaviors and steps for using the principles to promote and develop excellence at work at the individual level. Part Three, "The Strategies of the Game," outlines strategies for operationalizing excellence and provides examples and models that show how to implement the principles organizationwide. Finally, in Part Four, "Winners of the Game: Case Studies of Excellent Companies," we look at companies that live by the standards of "excellence at work" and that have, as a result, achieved recognition and success.

I suggest that while reading this book you keep an *Excellence Journal* in which you record your thoughts, ideas, examples and inspirations. You may find that you will continue to use an *Excellence Journal* for the rest of your working life as a reminder of your significant accomplishments and as a way of maintaining a strong commitment to excellence.

So, go ahead. Get in the game!

The Six Principles of Excellence
and What They Can Do for Your Organization

Each Excellence principle has a unique set of ground rules, activities, strategies and real-world examples to help your company achieve better results.

Table 1-1:

The Six Principles of Excellence

The Principle	The Result
Use Your Word Wisely *You communicate with quality and integrity in a way that inspires others to action.*	Promotes productive, future-focused communication that inspires results and encourages positivity.
Be Accountable *You are proactive and passionate, even in the toughest circumstances.*	Fosters proactive, responsible behaviors, including risk taking, truth telling and empowerment, that speed up decision-making, reduce conflict and improve business results.
Focus *You align your daily actions and behaviors with what matters most.*	Aligns individual actions and behaviors with corporate and team goals in order to increase effective use of time and focus and increase employee satisfaction.
Mine the Gold *You bring out the best in yourself and others.*	Improves collaboration, enhances internal and external customer service and leverages individual strengths that help employees realize their full potential and develop increased loyalty to the organization.
Strive for Balance *You are vital and energetic as a result of a balanced life.*	Improves work–life balance, which increases employee engagement and workplace wellness.
Lighten Up *You remember not to take yourself so seriously.*	Safeguards against burnout, increases employee morale and creates an environment in which employees thrive.

part 1

Getting in the Game

chapter 1

A New Paradigm for the Workplace

*"Independent of others and in concert with others,
your main task in life is to do what you can best do
and become what you can potentially be."*

—Erich Fromm

"It was the best of times, it was the worst of times." Charles Dickens's words could aptly be applied to today's business environment. Some companies will find innovative and creative ways to meet the challenges that the next two decades present, and they will thrive. Others, especially those that rely on traditional hierarchies and rigid linear thinking, will not.

Some observers point to recent trends and events in the business world and shake their heads. Economist Simon Head analyzed the corporate environment of call centers and managed medical practices in his book *The Ruthless New Economy.* He found that "reengineering" had demoralized and degraded workers through micromanagement, scripted software and a "Big Brother is watching you" mentality, which—as it turns out—isn't even cost-effective.

The high cost of glamorous but ineffective CEOs and CFOs is also cited as a sign of the decline and fall of American business. And while the scandals of Enron and Tyco made yesterday's news headlines, other scandals that leave investors with empty pockets continue to be uncovered.

It's a New World

Companies that ignore the importance of human capital management and fail to develop a comprehensive, integrated "employer-of-choice" strategy will be vulnerable as the United States faces its biggest labor crisis in its history.

The United States Chamber of Commerce noted that with the retirement of 77 million baby boomers, the country is facing a staggering worker shortage in the first quarter of this century. The chamber cited Census Bureau data that estimates the nation will need an additional 20 million workers to sustain economic growth between 2000 and 2026. Employment demand is projected to outstrip workforce growth.

In "New Realities in Today's Workforce," Towers Perrin reported figures that are even more alarming: "Workforce demographics are changing by every measure: gender, race, national origin, religion, age and so on. Simultaneously, a shortage of top talent is emerging. According to the U.S. Bureau of Labor Statistics, our organizations will need to fill 55 million positions over the next decade, but only 29 million employees will be available. This 26 million shortfall will affect all employers."

The challenge facing business leaders is to find and retain good employees and then optimize their value and retain them. To succeed, they must inspire those employees to do their very best and to achieve the levels of excellence that will be required to compete in a global marketplace.

In his book, *The Whole New Mind*, Daniel H. Pink addressed the fact that in many parts of the world, especially India, workers now have learned the "left-brained" analytical skills that in the past gave midlevel American workers an advantage. There will thus continue to be a flow of certain types of work to other countries. However, Pink also heralded the coming of "the conceptual age" to replace the information-driven age. He described the conceptual age as being "animated by a different form of thinking and a new approach to life." He and others have asserted that qualities such as creativity, joy, playfulness and empathy will determine "who flourishes and who flounders."

The Multigenerational Workforce

Workforce demographics are changing. For the past three decades, the workplace has been dominated by the baby boomers. A one-size-fits-all approach to management has been the rule. In the next decade, employers will need to adapt to meet the unique needs and demands of a variety of generations, each with its own mindset and expectations of the employment experience.

The millennial generation (those born between 1980 and 2000) brings a new set of values to the table. These people are competitive and achievement-oriented, but also civic-minded and diverse. They thrive in a structured environment, and they are gifted multitaskers. As employees, they value honesty and integrity in their leaders. They need to be challenged, and they look for a fun, irreverent workplace. (Think Google!) For this group of workers, work-life balance is a key issue, and employers ignore it at their own peril. The way to retain these workers is through rapid rewards, highly creative work and face-to-face interactions with managers.

Members of Generation X (those born between 1960 and 1980) are independent and entrepreneurial. They are mobile and flexible, and they expect honesty, visual stimulation and variety. They learn by doing, they focus on results and they desire immediate feedback (e.g., video games). These workers look for signs of employer commitment before they develop loyalty. For them, commitment is a two-way street.

The baby boomers (those born between 1943 and 1960) are expected not to retire in droves. Many of them have no intention of leaving the workforce. However, they can be expected to move to second or even third careers as they seek opportunities for emotional fulfillment and meaning in their lives. The baby boomers believe achievement is a result of paying one's dues and are willing to mentor others to success. They believe in teamwork, group discussion and duty, and they gladly accept increased responsibility.

The Excellence principles are well-suited to the next generation of workers as well as to Generation X and baby boomers because they are based on a fundamental human desire that we all share: to be our best. We all want to contribute, add value and live fulfilling lives. By incorporating creativity, rapid reward, integrity and fun, the principles help workers experience job satisfaction and sustained passion for their work.

Excellence is Part of a Total Rewards Strategy

Savvy employers who subscribe to the Total Rewards philosophy understand that the Excellence principles are an invaluable tool for implementation of a Total Rewards model. From both a theoretical and a practical approach, these principles align with the goals of attraction, motivation and retention that are central to the model.

The concept of total rewards emerged in the 1990s as a new way of thinking about the deployment of compensation and benefits. This new way of thinking combined compensation and benefits with the other tangible and intangible ways that companies seek to attract, motivate and retain employees. Total rewards is the monetary and nonmonetary return provided to employees in exchange for their time, talents, efforts and results.

It has become increasingly clear that the battle for talent involves much more than highly effective, strategically designed compensation and benefits programs. While these programs remain critical, the most successful companies have realized that they must take a much broader look at the factors involved in attraction, motivation and retention. And they must deploy all of the factors—including compensation, benefits, work–life, performance and recognition, and development and career opportunities—in order to achieve strategic advantage.

While workers in the past may have been satisfied with a good wage and comprehensive benefits package, today's employees demand much more. They want to be well compensated, feel valued, be recognized and given ample opportunity to enjoy work-life flexibility. And, equally as important, they want to work in a good environment and have a positive employment experience.

While compensation and benefits certainly play key roles in talent attraction, motivation and retention, they may be determined by factors outside your control as a manager or leader. However, the elements of work-life balance, performance and recognition, and development and career opportunities are areas over which you have direct influence. The Excellence principles give you the tools with which you can affect these areas and take continuous action to maximize employee performance.

Excellence is Values-Based

Patricia Aburdene claimed in her book *Megatrends 2010: The Rise of Conscious Capitalism* that we are at the dawning of a more conscious capitalism. The flagrant abuses in which some companies have indulged succeeded in awakening others to the need for integrity, strong ethics and spirituality in the workplace. "Today we are birthing a new and wiser version of capitalism, one that reconciles profit with the values we hold dear," she wrote.

The principles presented in this book are "values-based" and will prove vital to those who are striving to achieve conscious capitalism. The principles are a vehicle for transformation of the workplace to a traditional values-based environment grounded in trust, respect and integrity.

We live in a time of extraordinary demand. People are demoralized by layoffs, downsizing, outsourcing and offshoring; they are re-examining their personal values in a search for greater meaning and fulfillment. Business has reached a critical nexus. To renew the spirit of their employees and continue to harness their genius, businesses today look at how the organization's values and consciousness are affecting employees. Some questions you might ask yourself and others:

• What are the values of our organization?
• Are these values aligned with my personal values?
• Are we being true to our values?
• Where are we missing the mark?

In a message to Spirit in Business, an organization devoted to inspiring and supporting visionary leaders in raising consciousness, capacity and performance, H.H. The Dalai Lama said, "At the present time, globalization and advances in

Figure 1-1

WorldatWork Total Rewards Model

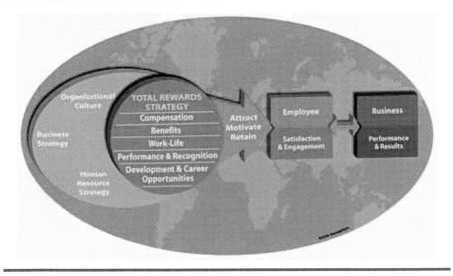

information technology have made our world so much smaller. This particularly applies to business leaders, whose actions have an impact on the lives of many people, both their employees and the customers they serve all over the world. Personally, I don't believe you need to be a religious or spiritual person to appreciate this reality and act accordingly. However, the world's religions all have in common an emphasis on developing qualities such as ethics, tolerance and compassion. Some people may think that these sort of ethical attitudes are not much needed within economic activity. I strongly disagree. The quality of all our actions depends on our motivation. In economics and business, as in all other fields of human activity, if you have a good motivation and seek to contribute to a better human society, you will be a good and honest businessman or economist."

American business has shown a remarkable ability to recreate itself, and an enormous pool of talented, diligent and innovative men and women occupy its ranks. Their talent and ingenuity is evident not just in new products and services but in the way we think about business. For example, in Charlotte, North Carolina, the McColl Center of the Visual Arts was co-founded by Hugh McColl, former chairman and CEO of Bank of America. In addition to serving the artistic community, the center has established the Innovation Institute, which trains executives to think like artists, to reinvigorate their creativity and to harness their imagination. The director has stated, "It is now necessary to lead in innovation instead of reacting to it." Executives, government leaders and others have responded enthusiastically.

The Courage to Excel

Sir Richard Branson, founder and CEO of Virgin companies (Virgin Airlines, Virgin Records and others) hosted an innovative reality TV show entitled "The Rebel Billionaire." The premise of the show is a group of young, bold business hopefuls who are competing in a series of challenges. The last man or woman standing has the opportunity to be the CEO of one of the Virgin companies.

In one particular episode, Branson took a team up in a hot-air balloon. Their task was to cross from one hot-air balloon to another by walking across a very narrow plank—at 10,000 feet from the ground.

Sara, a young entrepreneur, openly admitted her overwhelming fear of heights and sheer terror about performing the task. Nevertheless, she refused to let her team down and, more importantly, was not willing to give up the chance of winning the game and becoming CEO of Virgin. After Sara watched her six teammates "walk the plank," it was her turn. As she got a third of the way across, she was told to return to the original basket since the fuel had run out and the balloon had to land immediately. By this time, she was in a pitiable state.

To determine whether she or the other remaining unsuccessful contestant would be sent home, Sara had to participate in a second challenge. The second challenge required the contestants to climb up a 150-foot free-floating rope ladder to the top of the hot-air balloon, which was still at 10,000 feet. When they reached the top, they would be treated to an English tea party with Sir Richard Branson and continue participating in the series.

It took an excruciating 30 minutes for Sara to climb the ladder, but eventually she reached the top of the hot-air balloon. When she got there, she was so exhilarated, so proud and so pumped up that she put her foot through the balloon fabric and almost fell 10,000 feet. But fortunately, she didn't.

In her quest for success, Sara demonstrated the courage to excel in every sense. She dug deep, perhaps deeper than she had ever dug in her life, to bring out the physical strength, mental focus and emotional clarity needed to perform the task. In so doing, she went way beyond where people would normally go to succeed, not because she had to—after all, this was just a game made up by a television producer—but because she was committed to being fully engaged in the game and being her unrestricted best. Not for one minute was she willing to give in to circumstance, let her team down or settle for anything less than her very best.

Most of us rarely challenge ourselves in unimaginable ways like Sara did. We get caught up in the day-to-day activities or routines of our lives and allow ourselves to settle for "average." We forget how exhilarating it is to push beyond our limits. How exciting it is when we ask more of ourselves! How fulfilling it is to excel!

Maximizing Potential, Inspiring Others

You might not be asking your employees to climb ladders 10,000 feet above the ground, but most businesses operate in a white-water environment. The pace is relentless, the workload crushing and the demands often overwhelming. These are the questions facing organizational leaders:

- How do I maximize employee potential?
- How do I engage every person in my company to be his or her unrestricted best, no matter the circumstances?
- How do I reinvigorate my employees, renew their commitment and refocus them on success?

Maximizing your employees' potential doesn't mean they work longer hours, bear more stress or suffer more burnout. They are probably already doing that very well.

An Internet travel company was recently bought by a big competitor, and the first change the new owners made was to cancel all vacation for their employees— a workforce that was already putting in 10- and 12-hour days to help with the transition. Those employees may be afraid in the short run to leave their positions, but you can bet they won't be working at their maximum potential. Eventually, the company's reputation and its bottom line will suffer.

Why is it so important to master the ability to bring out the best in your workforce? According to a 2003 study by the Brookings Institute (www.brookings.edu), the primary source of market value in organizations has changed radically in the past few decades. When the study began in 1982, tangible assets such as machinery, product, buildings and so forth made up 62 percent of an organization's market value. The other 38 percent came from intangible assets, which include brand, intellectual property and *the quality of the workforce*. In 20 years, these numbers were reversed. Today, approximately 80 percent of market value for most organizations lies in its intangible assets.

Unlocking Potential

Traditional thought suggests that we use only about 10 percent of our capacity. Robert K. Cooper asserts in his book, *The Other 90%: How to Unlock Your Vast Untapped Potential for Leadership & Life*, that we use only one ten-thousandth of our capabilities. Imagine inspiring your employees to use one more ten-thousandth of their capabilities. What a unique perspective to hold when asking yourself, "How can I improve productivity and yield better results?" Your employees will become more productive workers, and all aspects of their lives will improve when they commit to excellence.

Most people are tired of just showing up every day and doing their jobs. They want more. They want to be engaged, alive and passionate about their work. People want to expand their capacity. They want to realize more of their potential. As a leader, your challenge is to unleash more of your employees' hidden capacity and inspire them to better leverage their strengths. Your mission is to send them home at the end of each day feeling proud, fulfilled and successful.

To achieve your mission, you have to give your workers the tools to self-manage. Then you must create an environment that inspires and demands excellence. When you integrate the Excellence principles into the work environment, those principles become a common language and shared commitment in your organization. They create a unique momentum and accountability for excellence, and enable you to create a high-performance environment.

The Formula for Achieving Excellence

Excellence is no longer an option. To succeed in today's business world, we have to be constantly looking for ways to add more value. Good enough isn't good enough! We are either in growth or we are in decay. There is no middle ground. The pathway to achieving excellence is simple. Excellence starts with our willingness to see the truth about the way things are and to then have the courage and discipline to establish new standards for ourselves and others in our organization. Doing this requires a willingness to see and create new pathways, and a profound commitment to participating fully with no boundaries, no fear and not settling for "the way we have always done it."

Everything that takes place in your organization is a reflection of its leaders. If you are not satisfied with the performance, morale and loyalty of your team, the question to ask yourself is: "Who am I being as a leader, and who do I need to be to inspire others to achieve excellence?" As a leader, Excellence begins and ends with you. Your success in achieving organizational excellence will require your unwavering commitment, laser-like persistence and utmost discipline. Above all, your every word and action should be the most inspiring expression of excellence.

When I speak with groups of managers, I am quick to remind them that their success is inevitably dependent on the success of their people. As a manager, it doesn't matter that you have an impressive title, a six-figure salary or a corner office. What matters is whether or not the people who work with and for you are realizing their fullest potential. This is the true sign of a successful leader. To get the best from people, it is important to establish basic ground rules for what is acceptable and what isn't. Think of these ground rules like a "playbook" for a sport or game.

The Excellence Code establishes such a set of ground rules and expectations. It is a set of principles that govern what constitutes excellent behavior within your organization. The code is a self-governing system designed to help people self-manage. Those that violate the code will be brought back into alignment by a system of peer accountability. As one client said, "It is impossible for us to go forward the way we were going to go forward. Once you are aware of these principles, you can no longer feel comfortable being anything less than your absolute best."

Figure 1-2:
The Excellence Code

- We lead from wherever we are.
- Every day we choose to be our unrestricted best.
- We think and speak possibility.
- We focus on what's working and what we want to see happen.
- We are proactive.
- We are always asking: "How can I achieve the best results?"
- We focus on what really matters.
- Our daily actions are a reflection of our deepest values and grandest goals.
- We seek to bring out more of the best in ourselves and others.
- We relate to others from the point of view of their unseen potential.
- We strive for optimal effectiveness in all areas of our life.
- We sustain high levels of energy, vitality and passion as a result of a balanced life.
- We remember not to take ourselves so seriously.
- We create a work environment filled with fun, humor and joy where we thrive.
- We remember excellence is just a state of mind put into action.

chapter 2

Defining Excellence

Excellent: very good of its kind: eminently good: first class.

—Merriam-Webster's Collegiate Dictionary,
Eleventh Edition

The word "excellence" means the state of being excellent. Excellence means many things to many people. To achieve excellence in your organization, you must first define it, and then give people the tools to distinguish and measure it. Whatever the definition you give it in your company, the ultimate purpose of that definition is to affirm great worth and ensure exceptional quality.

The Excellence principles are universal truths that have been taught for decades. As a student of the Excellence principles, my commitment is to guide others in their discovery of excellence and to relentlessly draw out their magnificence. Such work often requires unusual compassion and patience.

Kevin, a sales manager, had received extremely negative feedback from his peers and direct reports. His staff said he was rude and aggressive, and that he made them feel stupid, unvalued and disrespected. In fact, two of his top performers who had recently quit said they were no longer willing to work for him. The feedback was obviously upsetting to Kevin, and he was understandably concerned about his future with the company. As is typical in a 360-degree feedback process, his initial reaction was to be defensive, to refuse to accept the feedback, to offer excuses and explanations to prove the comments were invalid, incorrect or had been provided by one or two of his employees who he knew did not like him. He went on and on for the first hour of our meeting, blaming others and refusing to take responsibility. Frankly, I wondered if there was any point in continuing the conversation.

But I pressed on, convinced I could help him move forward and use the feedback in a productive and meaningful way. I had to mine the gold. This meant that rather than telling him what he needed to do and how to do it—why he needed to get off his high horse and stop making others wrong so he could be right—I listened appreciatively for ways to bring out the best of what he might have to offer. I shifted the focus away from the past, the historical explanations and the excuses and focused on the future.

These are the kinds of questions I asked him:

- How do you want to move forward from here?
- What can you do to change others' perceptions?
- What is your vision for yourself and your team?
- What would be possible if you "owned" this feedback and made some positive changes?

As he focused on the future, he opened up to new ideas. By the end of our session, he had made a commitment to address the feedback and seek out the necessary resources to make adjustments in his management style. What a stunning reversal! I had helped to bring out the best in him and successfully gained his commitment to taking a different approach to his relationships with his team—an approach that would bring out the best in them and at the same time create a sense of loyalty.

Just as when Michelangelo was tasked with creating David, he began with a large block of marble, and for months he chipped away relentlessly at the unwanted pieces until the shape of David was revealed, your role as a leader is to be the architect of your employee's success. Michelangelo demonstrated the ability to create a masterpiece from a block of marble. It took vision, commitment and mastery to chip away at all the unwanted stone and extract a work of art. The job of a leader is similar. Great managers and leaders have mastered the art of bringing out the best in people. They practice their art by helping people where they could be more effective and by then engaging them in the improvement process.

The Excellence Thermostat

I once participated in a workshop on how to create wealth. One of the first questions the presenter asked was: "Where is your internal wealth thermostat set?" Where our thermostat is set determines the amount of wealth we attract and manifest in our lives. If our thermostat is set fairly low, when we think about dollars, we think in hundreds. Example: "Wouldn't it be great if I received an unexpected gift or a rebate for a few hundred bucks?"

Other people may set their wealth thermostat a little higher. When they think of dollars, they think of thousands. Example: "I hope I get a few thousand dollars back from the IRS and can pay off a credit card."

Then, for some people, the wealth thermostat is set really high. When they think of dollars, they think of billions. These are the Bill Gateses, the Donald Trumps and the Rockefellers of the world. They have high expectations and a compelling vision for wealth, and thus they attract and manifest a lot of money.

In the same way that our wealth thermostat determines how much money we create, our Excellence Thermostat determines the amount of excellence we create. Where we set our Excellence Thermostat as individuals and for our organizations determines the level of excellence we achieve. Notice that I am referring to a "thermostat" rather than a "thermometer." A thermostat is something that you control. You decide where your thermostat is set. A thermometer, on the other hand, responds to the environment and is an effect of external conditions. This is an important distinction. The thermostat may fluctuate slightly with peaks of exceptionally high performance and lulls of low energy, but it always recalibrates to the programmed setting. The level of excellence we expect from ourselves and others will almost always determine our level of performance and productivity. We inevitably manage ourselves to achieve our beliefs. Therefore, if we raise our Excellence Thermostat setting, it follows that we will hold ourselves and others to higher standards.

Read the low and high markers in Figure 2-1 on page 24 and then take a moment to establish where your Excellence Thermostat is now set and how that setting is affecting you and your organization. (Feel free to amend and fine-tune the descriptors as appropriate to your particular circumstances.)

Low Excellence Thermostat Settings
Do you recognize any of these behaviors in yourself or your team?
- You feel fragmented, stressed and burned out.
- You are overwhelmed and frustrated with your workload.
- A light glaze of resignation and cynicism has settled over your eyes.
- You come to work every day, you do your work, you might even work long hours, but you are doing so without enthusiasm and just going through the motions.
- Most of your conversations during the workday are focused on what's not working, what ought to be fixed and "ain't it awful."
- You often find yourself blaming others, pointing fingers and wishing someone would take care of the problems.
- You believe there is nothing you can really do to make a difference anymore.
- Although you are extremely busy and may even feel tired and stressed at the end of a day, you often feel that you haven't really accomplished anything of

Figure 2-1

Excellence Thermostat Settings

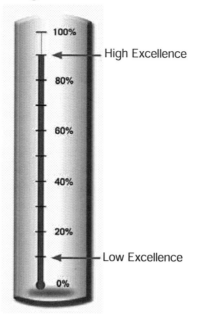

High Excellence

Low Excellence

Excellence Thermostat

great importance, and you thus feel a lack of fulfillment and satisfaction.

- You find it takes a lot of time and energy to get things done simply because there is a lack of collaboration, cooperation and shared commitment to the common goal.
- At times you feel you are dragging, your energy level is low and vitality is lacking; you have thus barely a spark of passion.
- Although your job is okay, you don't feel as if you are thriving, and you can't remember when you last bounced out of bed, skipped your caffeine burst and bolted into work brimming with enthusiasm.

High Excellence Thermostat Settings

Now let's look at how we think and behave when our Excellence Thermostat is set high:

- You are fully engaged, passionate and inspired.
- Your communication is impeccable; every conversation you have forwards the action powerfully.
- You are proactive, always owning, resolving and acting on issues, without excuses.

- You use your time and energy wisely and effectively to produce extraordinary results. As a result, at the end of each day you have a deep sense of accomplishment.
- You are a master at influencing people. They collaborate, cooperate and work together in harmony.
- Your energy level is consistently high, and you are vital and vibrant in every way.
- You love your work and you are thriving.

One way that I know my Excellence Thermostat is set high is when I drift off to sleep at the end of a day and my last few thoughts are this or something similar: "I am masterful. Today I achieved extraordinary results with integrity, grace and ease. I am proud and moved by my accomplishments. I am excelling in ways I had not dreamed possible."

When did you last have these thoughts as you drifted off to sleep?

When our Excellence Thermostat is set high, we are tapped in, tuned in and turned on, and nothing will stop us from being the very best we can be. When our thermostat is set low, we waste time, lose energy, perform at low levels and are disengaged.

Why is it important to identify the Excellence Thermostat setting in your workplace? The first thing to realize is that attitudes and behaviors are contagious. They run rampant in organizations. Sometimes management tries to ignore the problems, believing they will disappear on their own. But that rarely happens, and in the meantime the negativity depletes people's energy, diminishes their ability to focus and erodes their trust. According to Loehr and Schwartz in *The Power of Full Engagement*, energy is the "fundamental currency of performance." When energy is low, it follows that productivity suffers.

Certainly, as a leader, or even as a member of a team, you would want to know the Excellence Thermostat setting of other people you work with. I know I always choose to be surrounded by people who are at the top of their game and are continuously challenging themselves to have breakthrough results. I recommend that reporting on the Excellence Thermostat setting be a regular activity on your team—each person candidly tells the group his or her Excellence Thermostat setting and his or her commitment to excellence.

No one wakes up in the morning and says, "Today my commitment is to be as lazy and mediocre as I can possibly be." We want to be and to do our best, if at all possible. When we are not able to live up to our potential and are not satisfied with our performance, conduct, results and the quality of our work life, the result is *disengagement*.

Activity Excellence Thermostat

In your Excellence Journal, write down today's date with your current Excellence Thermostat setting on a scale of 0 percent to 100 percent. The accuracy of the number you write down is less important than the fact that you continue to ask yourself where your Excellence Thermostat is set and that you consider its effect.

Are you satisfied with your current Excellence Thermostat setting?

_____

_____

If you are not excelling at the level you would like to, or know you are capable of, how does that affect you? How does it affect your organization?

_____

_____

Now, identify where the Excellence Thermostat is set in your team, department or organization.

_____

_____

How does your Excellence Thermostat setting influence your team's setting?

_____

_____

What level of excellence are you committed to?

_____

_____

What do you think it would take to achieve and sustain the level of excellence to which you say you are committed?

_____

_____

The Cost of Disengagement

Disengagement is the state of being uninterested, unenthusiastic and unmotivated. When employees are disengaged, they do not enjoy their work and do not feel valued for their contributions. The problem is epidemic in many organizations.

Research by Development Dimensions International (DDI) reveals that only 19 percent of employees are highly engaged. The Corporate Executive Board, a network for leaders of the world's largest public and private organizations, examined levels of engagement across 50,000 employees around the world and placed only 11 percent in what it called the "true believer" category. Towers Perrin's recent "Talent Report" is slightly more optimistic, finding just 17 percent of the 35,000 employees surveyed to be highly engaged.

The Gallup organization reported that in the United States, up to 70 percent of employees are disengaged *The Gallup Management Journal's* 2006 Q2 survey found that of all U.S. workers 18 or older, about 20.6 million—or roughly 15 percent—are actively disengaged. Gallup estimates that the lower productivity of actively disengaged workers costs the U.S. economy about $328 billion annually.

When I was working with a group of high-level directors in a technology company, the 18 executives in the group calculated the cost of disengagement on the part of their teams to be in excess of $2.5 million per year. What do you think the cost is to your team, department or organization? In the next chapter you will have the opportunity to calculate this cost.

What can you do?

The Excellence Thermostat setting in your organization is a reflection of you (as a leader). That is, the level of excellence in your organization is a reflection of the standards and expectations you have of yourself and of others. If you are satisfied with the level of excellence in your company, that's great. If not, you will want to inquire as to what your role is in the matter.

Here are some questions to consider in your *Excellence Journal*:

- How do you define excellence?
- What does excellence look like, sound like and feel like?
- What are the signs that excellence is present?

As you think about your answers, go beyond the traditional definitions of completion of the task or delivery of the product on time and on budget.

- If what you define as excellence were present consistently, what would it look like?

Raise Awareness of Your Organization's Thermostat Setting

Rob noticed that his company's Excellence Thermostat setting was lower than he'd like it to be. There was "a ton of turnover," and "everyone had a huge to-do list," but they were not accomplishing anything except the bare minimum. The cost, he felt, was evident in the lost opportunities.

"We could be doing so much," he said. "I've been in my position for almost a year. I used to get in by 6:30 a.m., and I felt excited about coming to work." But he was no longer excited. He hadn't realized it, however, until he thought about the setting of his organization's Excellence Thermostat.

You can raise awareness of your organization's level of excellence by first explaining the concept behind the Excellence Thermostat and then placing a graphic of the thermostat where it will be visible to others in the organization. At the beginning of meetings, set aside a few minutes to discuss excellence and where your organization's rating is at the particular time. This brings the idea of excellence to the forefront of people's minds.

- What kind of experience would you, your co-workers, customers and vendors have if excellence were present? What would be the atmosphere in your workplace?

Exceptional leadership is a known "engagement driver" in the workplace. According to Wellins et al., "Leaders have the influence and power to serve as catalysts for higher levels of engagement, not only in one or two areas, but in all aspects of leadership."

DDI's assessment and testing research showed that:

- More engaged managers have more engaged direct reports.
- The direct reports of engaged managers are less likely to leave the organization.
- Higher-performing managers have direct reports who are more highly engaged.

Through training and through rigorous adherence to the Excellence principles, you can have a positive effect on employee engagement. DDI studies showed that when leaders improved their skills through training, employees became more engaged in their work.

Excellence is Never an Accident

We don't wake up one day and discover ourselves to be in a state of excellence. It is rigorously planned, relentlessly practiced, consistently role modeled, agreed on, tracked and measured.

Excellence is a consciousness, a way of thinking, speaking and relating to others and our environment that gives us power and energy. We want to excel, because it is evident that in doing so the quality of our work life and our personal life will improve.

Why, then, does it seem so difficult to achieve and sustain excellence? What are the barriers or blocks? In the story about Kevin, his attainment of excellence was blocked by his poor communication skills and his lack of accountability for the effect his behaviors had on others—common barriers to excellence. In the next chapter we'll take a closer look at these and other barriers to excellence and what they cost your company.

Figure 2-2:

Qualities of Excellence

- We insist on the highest standards.
- We expect the very best of others and ourselves.
- We constantly challenge the status quo.
- We don't settle for yesterday's definition of excellence.

chapter 3

Barriers to Excellence

"You get the best effort from others not by lighting a fire beneath them but by building a fire within them."

—Bob Nelson

Tom works as the head of manufacturing at a major research and development corporation. The company has two facilities, one for design and development and one for production. Tom has many responsibilities, one of which is to serve as a liaison between the two facilities. Early on in his role, Tom ran into a number of stumbling blocks.

"The biggest problem," he explains, "was that of perception. The people at the two facilities eyed each other with suspicion. They were competitive rather than cooperative, and each group seemed to think the grass was greener at the other facility." Instead of behaving like a team, the employees were fragmented.

Tom noticed that routine meetings quickly degenerated into "moan and groan" sessions. A victim mentality had infiltrated the workforce, and employees were focused on what was wrong instead of what was right. Whenever there was a problem, employees reacted as if the sky were falling.

Tom's company, obviously, had several barriers to excellence. Over the years, I have observed these and other barriers again and again, and I've identified six of the most common barriers to excellence. This is not an exhaustive list. There are barriers specific to your organization that you can add. But this group of barriers is a sound starting point.

As you read over the barriers in this section, note which of them exist in your organization and then estimate the average number of hours per week you or your co-workers spend on these behaviors.

Unproductive Communication

Conversations that take place out loud, via e-mail, voice mail or silently inside our heads that are negative and unproductive, including gossip, criticism, complaints and other conversations that don't lead anywhere except to more resignation and cynicism.

How much time in an average week is spent on these kinds of conversations?

Nonaccountability

Nonaccountable behaviors include pointing fingers, blaming others, holding back and refusing to speak the truth. The result is that you have to put out fires, handle "dropped balls" and investigate breakdowns.

How much time in an average week is spent on these kinds of activities?

Lack of Focus

With all the demands we face at work, we often find ourselves not being fully present to people. We feel fragmented and distracted, and we are therefore not able to effectively execute on priorities. We make unwise use of our time and energy, and the result is that we feel fatigued and stressed.

How much time in an average week is wasted due to lack of focus?

Poor Interpersonal Relationships

When people work together, there is typically a buildup of friction caused by unresolved issues, conflict, differences and history. The result: a lack of collaboration, teamwork and cooperation, and limited opportunity for others to succeed.

How much time in an average week is wasted due to poor interpersonal relationships?

Low Energy and Vitality Due to Imbalance

With the frenetic pace of life and grueling demands we face, our lives tend to get out of balance. There is less time for recovery and renewal, and more opportunity for burnout and stress. The result: illness, absence and other stress-related issues.

How much time in an average week is lost due to physical, mental or emotional problems, including time absent from work and stress-related issues?

Absence of Joy

As our organizations are forced to become more competitive and as pressures increase, it seems as if the joy of work is compromised. We allow ourselves less freedom to have fun, laugh and enjoy work. Instead, we take ourselves far too seriously, and the result is burnout and low morale.

How much time in an average week is lost (or compromised) due to burnout and low morale?

One more very important and costly barrier to excellence is an unwillingness to lead: our unwillingness or the unwillingness of people in our organizations to lead from wherever they are. The resulting inertia can be expensive, and it serves in a powerful way to discourage excellence.

Take a minute to think about the barriers to excellence in your organization. Avoid mentioning or pointing fingers at external influences and circumstances. Systems and processes can certainly represent barriers, but remember, we are the creators of our circumstances. Look at the behaviors and factors that you can control. Perhaps in your organization there are additional barriers you believe are a source of disengagement. Feel free to add these and estimate the time lost due to these issues.

The total estimated cost of unproductive behavior to a company of 1,000

Figure 3-1:

Calculating the Cost of Barriers

The barriers to excellence prevent people from focusing on what's really important and from being productive. Use the following formula to calculate the annual cost of these "productivity blocks" to your organization.

STEP 1:
Number of employees x average hourly wage:
For example, 1,000 employees x $25 per hour = $25,000

STEP 2:
Average # of productivity hours* lost each week x cost of labor:
For example, 15 hours x $25,000 cost of labor = $75,000
*It is estimated that on average employees lose at least 3 hours per day
(or 15 hours per week) due to productivity blocks.

STEP 3:
Cost per year:
For example, $75,000 per week x 52 weeks = $3,900,000

---

employees is $3.9 million. At a time when most companies are looking for ways to cut corners and increase savings, imagine if you were able to reduce this cost by just 10 percent? Typically, companies get stuck in the old paradigm of cutting back on positions, controlling overhead spending, freezing merit increases or foregoing training and development. These approaches contribute to deeper disengagement and decreased productivity. The new model is to engage, educate and inspire people to commit to excellence.

As for Tom's company, the leadership knew something had to be done. We implemented the Excellence principles at the leadership level and for line employees. I'll let Tom describe the results:

I saw the barriers start to break down. You just don't turn a switch. You have to practice, but as we began to focus on changing habits, we began practicing being better people overall.

I've noticed in a lot of the meetings that people avoid the downward spiral. They try to present a problem as an opportunity with a solution instead of as "the sky is falling." Now, they're looking for confirmation to act on the solution. Communication is more relaxed, less guarded. Previously, people always felt they had to guard every word they said. But in a team environment they can say what they think, and they can say things constructively.

Another principle that really helps us is "Mining the Gold." People started realizing that everybody brings certain resources to the team. Not everybody has to bring the same attributes. It's a synergy of individuals. Employees are now more accepting of the fact that people bring in different skill sets, and it's necessary. When you're in a manufacturing environment, you have certain craftsmen with certain skills—you realize that particular skill is handy ... Sometimes people would get caught up in the fact that not everyone has an aerospace background. But I think now they see that people are able to draw on prior experience. We hired a guy who used to paint custom cars. He became a fabulous airplane painter. He didn't have an aerospace background, but the craftsmanship applies.

The other principle that really drove home was "Be Accountable." People were feeling like victims and looking for sympathy. When they got out of that mode, they were able to see that even the small details are important. People get caught up in thinking that they want to make one big impact, but that doesn't happen very often. It's the people who take care of the little things that enable the big picture to happen. If you are accountable at your end of it, it helps the whole picture flow together ... I have 250 people reporting to me, and I need to know the people out there are doing their jobs. It's impor-

tant that they're accountable in all their day-to-day activities. You can lose a lot over something that seems small. For example, everything that comes in to us has to have safety records. If a painter, for instance, is being accountable, then everything in his area is handled safely, and that translates to savings at a corporate level.

Now, the flow of information is constructive. People aren't worried about "them" or "us" anymore. Once people start realizing they have roles in the big picture, then they're not competing against each other anymore. That's excellence.

chapter 4

Cultivating the Habit of Excellence

Kirk participated in the Excellence program some time ago. An engineer, he had an analytical, "yes but, what if, how about" kind of attitude and debated with me on just about every point I made. His resistance to the topic was obvious, but I also sensed some underlying sadness and disappointment.

He approached me at the end of the day, shook my hand and with great emotion told me how much he had enjoyed the program. I almost fell over in amazement (and relief). Then he told me his story.

Kirk had been a manager for years. He had participated in nearly every management, leadership and personal-development seminar that was available. He had listened to all the tapes and read all the books. He knew every theory and every strategy. There was nothing new you could tell him about the subject. Despite all this, he told me, he still felt like he was overworked and underpaid. He was frustrated, resigned and cynical. His team was still dysfunctional, wasted inordinate amounts of time on "urgent" but unimportant issues and was burned out. His manager, he had come to realize, was never going to change. As for the organization, it was like many other organizations—dysfunctional and substandard.

What Kirk realized for the very first time as he learned the Excellence principles was that until he changed the way he thought, spoke, interacted with others and managed himself, his circumstances were not going to change. He realized that excellence is a frame of mind that alters the fundamental way you go about your business every day. He also realized that excellence does not happen as a result of sitting in a seminar, reading a book, listening to a tape or dreaming of what you would like to see happen. Excellence happens as a result of radical commitment to practicing new habits in order to get new results.

The Clean Source

You probably have days, or perhaps weeks and months, when you find yourself just coasting along in mediocrity. For the most part, no one really notices or confronts our mediocrity, but we know. We know we can be more productive and effective. But it seems that when we get up in the morning, we get caught up in the whirl of life and often find ourselves unconsciously just going through the motions, not ever really excelling in the way we know is possible.

We need to remember that excellence is a state of mind. It's a choice we make every day—sometimes every hour or even every moment—to look outward, onward and upward in new ways and to challenge ourselves to realize more of our potential.

Excellence is a consciousness—a way in which we think, speak, relate to others and manage our response to the environment—that gives us more power and greater fulfillment, and therefore, more success. It is a source of energy and vitality.

Excellence is a result of consistent practice, like adding drops of clean water to a dirty bucket of water. If you consistently add clean water to the bucket, eventually the dirty water is eliminated, and what you have is a clear, clean source. When we work and live from that clean source, everything is possible!

Streamline

When I was a little girl in first grade, I was on the swim team. I loved to compete and was delighted when the swim coach informed the team that our final competitive event would be in an Olympic-sized pool. Of course, when you are little, you think you can do anything, and I was certain I would not only make it to the other side but I would win the race. Halfway across the pool, I started to flail and gasp for air. I flapped around, expending huge amounts of energy to stay afloat, all the while feeling increasingly humiliated as I realized I was dead last!

As you can imagine, my defeat was a defining moment in my life. Now more than 40 years later, I can still remember every detail of that day. After the embarrassment had worn off, I became very interested in what it took to be a champion swimmer. Why was it that some swimmers effortlessly glided to the finish, barely creating a ripple behind them? I watched with fascination as Olympic swimmer Mark Spitz swam with grace and precision, his movements smooth and artful, almost like a ballet dancer's performance. Spitz had mastered the art of streamlining—contouring his body to offer the least resistance and thus achieving a fluid flow. Although I didn't aspire to become an Olympic swimmer, over time I learned to streamline, and my swimming improved greatly. In fact, I was on the A team through my high school years.

The art of Excellence is similar. When we "streamline," we approach our work with fluidity and grace, minimizing the resistance caused by the unproductive behaviors discussed in the previous chapter. When we eliminate the barriers to excellence, we are able to achieve our goals with ease.

It's not what you do, it's how you do it

Excellence is not about what you do. It's about how you do it. Many companies can do what your company does. What distinguishes you is the way in which you execute and deliver.

For instructors at the community-college level, it is quite obvious when they are excelling. As a veteran teacher told me, "The curriculum is standard. It's the same old, same old content. How we deliver the material is what distinguishes us and encourages students to enroll in our classes. If my class enrollment is low, it is a clear sign for me that I have lost sight of the 'how' and I am focusing only on the 'what.'" In an environment like a community college, confirmation of excellence is immediate.

We get so caught up in the doing of things that we forget that the way in which we do what we do is as important, if not more important, than what we do. But, because it's the doing that seemingly determines the bottom line, we have allowed ourselves to neglect the manner in which we do things, and we are willing to tolerate behaviors in others and ourselves that are questionable.

When we go about our day-to-day lives with clarity, positivity, integrity, accountability, focus, passion, engagement, respect and kindness, we become more productive and more efficient. Isn't it ironic, then, that people will tell us they don't have time to practice excellence because they need to focus on the bottom line?

Remember, Excellence is just a habit!

Strategies for Implementing Excellence

- *Role Model Excellence*
  Consistently role model the Excellence principles. Be the kind of leader that when people think of you, they think of integrity, inspiration and passion.
- *Get Buy-in to Excellence*
  Enroll others in your vision for excellence. Gain their agreement and buy-in to the new code of conduct—not because they have to, but because they want to.
- *Train Others in Excellence*
  Give your people the opportunity to discover and master the six Excellence principles in a neutral environment. We have discovered that employees are

always more open to this kind of information when it comes from someone other than their managers.

- *Implement Systems to Support Excellence*

  Use the practical ideas in this book to implement new systems and processes that can create the context for sustained excellence.

- *Manage and Coach Excellence*

  Infuse your daily management and coaching practices with the Excellence principles. Talk about excellence at every opportunity that presents itself.

- *Acknowledge and Reward Excellence*

  You get the behavior you reward. Therefore, it is important that you consistently acknowledge and reward every demonstration of Excellence.

part 2

The Principles, or The Rules of the Game

The 6 Principles of Excellence

These six simple yet powerful principles form a code of conduct and shared commitment that inspires excellence.

1 Use Your Word Wisely

You communicate with quality and integrity in a way that inspires action.

The first and most fundamental principle of excellence has the power to transform your workplace. When you use your word wisely, you communicate powerfully and effectively in a way that influences others and inspires positivity and committed action.

2 Be Accountable

You are proactive and passionate, even in the toughest circumstances.

When you are accountable, you have the desire and confidence to be more proactive, to resolve breakdowns more effectively and to feel more in control of your circumstances.

3 Focus
You align your daily actions and behaviors with what matters most.

Excellence isn't magic or hocus pocus; it's simply learning how to focus. When you clarify what really matters, you are able to make the best use of your time and energy so that you can achieve your goals and have a greater sense of accomplishment.

4 Mine the Gold
You bring out the best in yourself and others.

Mining the gold offers a new approach to managing your relationships in order to foster increased collaboration and cooperation. Mining the gold also enhances your ability to easily and productively get things done through and with others.

5 Strive for Balance
You are vital and energetic as a result of a balanced life.

This principle gives you tools to achieve optimal effectiveness in all areas of your life—physical, intellectual, emotional, relational and spiritual—so that you maintain good work-life balance and enjoy consistently high levels of energy and vitality.

6 Lighten Up
You remember not to take yourself so seriously.

The "lighten up" principle reminds you to bring humor and lightness to your work and encourages you to create a fun, enjoyable work environment in which you and others thrive.

1 Use Your Word Wisely

You communicate with quality and integrity in a way that inspires action.

chapter 5

Principle 1: Use Your Word Wisely

*"The word is not just a sound or a written symbol.
The word is a force; it is the power you have
to express and communicate, to think,
and thereby to create the events of your life."*

— don Miguel Ruiz, *The Four Agreements*

Early one morning, I planned to start my day by exercising at the gym and getting into a positive state of mind in preparation for several meetings. As I began my workout, a woman was telling a friend about the recent spate of burglaries in the neighborhood. As others came and went, she repeated the story and succeeded in getting everyone upset, fearful and worried. After a few minutes, I felt angry and negative. Realizing how dramatically the negative conversation had affected me, and how that would affect the rest of my day, I left the gym just five minutes into my workout.

Use Your Word Wisely is the first and most fundamental principle of excellence. When you master this principle, it can transform your work environment. This principle will give you tools you can use to communicate more powerfully in a way that inspires others to action.

The Power of Your Word

Every word you think, speak or write has power. For example, when you turn on the TV and watch the local news reports highlighting the depressing, awful, violent things that happened that day, how do you generally feel and act? It's likely that you feel stressed, depressed, worried, unhappy, cynical, resigned and frustrated.

On the other hand, when you are with a group of inspired, positive people who are talking about great things, stimulating events and beautiful places, how do you generally feel? In this case, you probably feel inspired, positive, enthusiastic, energized and motivated to take powerful action.

Every conversation either strengthens us or weakens us. The words we use stimulate our emotions, which in turn influence our behavior, thereby creating either positive or negative circumstances and events in our lives. The power you have in your world depends on the quality of your communication. The greater the quality and integrity of your thinking and speaking, the more powerful you are.

Words in the Workplace

What is the quality of communication in your organization? Is communication clear, honest and precise, delivered with utmost integrity and designed to inspire others to take action? Or is the majority of conversation in your organization about what's not working, what ought to be fixed, gossip and general, negative chit-chat?

Most "hallway conversations" are dominated by complaints, gossip and general negativity. Often these conversations are tempered by humor, intelligence and rationality, but that doesn't mean they don't have a negative effect. They do. They keep people focused on the problems rather than on finding solutions and producing results.

When you use your word wisely, in every sense, you are focused on moving forward, producing results and delivering your very best. On the other hand, when you are engaged in downward spiral thinking and speaking, you are distracted, frustrated and fatigued—and your performance suffers.

To help make good communication a habit, you must establish systems and processes that support and encourage the wise use of words.

The Downward Spiral

When I was at the gym and the women got caught up in the fear and negativity of crime, they went into a "downward spiral." The downward spiral comes in many forms—some obvious, some not. Contributors to the downward spiral can include the following:

- The voice inside our heads, the downward spiral on "mute"; this type of downward spiral can be insidious
- Any and all conversations that are negative (e.g., that focus on what's not working, what ought to be fixed, "ain't it awful," nothing is ever going to change, I can't make a difference)

Figure 5-1:

New Ground Rules for Improved Communication

- We speak with kindness and respect, always.
- We contribute only thoughts and ideas that will help people take action.
- We offer opinions with the understanding they are not necessarily "the truth."
- We have no need to defend ourselves or our opinions.
- We listen appreciatively, without judgment.
- We focus on what's possible.
- We never make assumptions.
- We don't take anything personally.

- Things we say that go against ourselves and others, such as judgments, opinions and criticism
- Gossip, negative watercooler chit-chat or, nowadays, e-mail chit-chat about who said and did what and your opinion on the matter
- The need to defend ourselves and be right—when we make other people wrong, we are elevated and "win."

Just how damaging can the downward spiral be? Consider the Enron scandal—a perfect illustration of how people and companies establish a habit of gossip, lies and dishonesty. Newspaper reports told us that Enron traders openly discussed manipulating the California power market, making jokes about stealing from customers during the Western energy crisis in 2000 and 2001.

According to transcripts of telephone calls filed with the Federal Energy Regulatory Commission, traders openly discussed creating congestion on transmission lines, taking generating units offline to pump up electricity prices and overall manipulation of the California power market. The transcripts contained profanity and comments about customers, such as the comment about " ... all the money you guys stole from those poor grandmothers of California." The Enron trader responds, "Yeah, Grandma Millie, man. But she's the one who couldn't figure out how to (expletive) vote on the butterfly ballot."

This behavior, in effect, becomes the "way we do things around here." It starts with one small lie or a break in integrity and then spirals into a habit.

If all the conversations in your company were taped and made available for public scrutiny, how well would you come across to a listener? Would you be proud or ashamed? The downward spiral is so insidious. The irony is that it has become so much a part of corporate life that it is difficult to distinguish. A leader using profanity

Activity Conversations

Do you recognize these kinds of downward-spiral conversations? Identify the five most common downward spiral conversations in your group, department or organization. In your Excellence Journal, write down the theme or the main topic of the conversation, such as, "We are underpaid," "Management doesn't trust us," "We don't have the adequate resources."

or making jokes at the expense of others (including customers) implies an acceptance for the behavior, and the rest of the company feels comfortable emulating it.

Time Spent on Downward Spiral

Downward spiral conversations, in many cases, become "business as usual." In other words, we get so used to hearing them and participating in them that we take them for granted and don't even think about their effect. For example, when you turn on the TV at night, what do you hear more of—downward spiral or possibility? When you read the newspaper this morning or checked the news on the Internet, what did you read more of—downward spiral or possibility? Downward spiral thinking and speaking has become so much a part of our lives that it becomes invisible, though it remains powerful.

How much time do you estimate that people in your organization spend on downward spiral thinking and speaking on an average each day?

The Cost of the Downward Spiral

Now that you have considered approximately how much time is spent on downward spiral, what do you think is the effect of this phenomenon? How does the downward spiral affect your performance, the way you feel and the success of your organization? Answers might include the following:

- Loss of energy
- Frustration
- Cynicism
- Negativity
- Bad attitude
- Conflict
- Lack of focus
- Low productivity
- Poor customer service
- Poor collaboration
- Lack of cooperation
- Low morale
- Resignation
- Gossip in the community.

Downward spiral thinking and speaking saps energy and stops the action. It is like a puncture in a tire that slowly depletes our time, energy, focus and positivity.

Reasons for the Downward Spiral

We can all agree the downward spiral is damaging. Then why do we do it? Why is the downward spiral so compelling, seductive and easy to get caught up in? Possible answers include the following:

- It offers a sense of community.
- It's easier to complain than to take action.
- We can be lazy.
- It can be interesting and exciting.
- We are so used to it that we don't even recognize it anymore.
- It has become a habit.
- It's fun.
- We get to be right and make others wrong.
- We want to vent our frustrations.
- It's what everyone else is doing, so we had better join in.

Identify the Downward Spiral

Sometimes the downward spiral is easy to identify. Use the list of the most common downward spiral conversations in your organization as a guide and try to be more

Excellent Strategy

At an aeronautical systems company, employees developed their own Excellence Code of Honor. The code was a synthesis of the Excellence principles and their LEAN manufacturing credo presented on a laminated tag on the back of their name badges—a constant reminder of their agreements and accountabilities to each other!

aware of these conversations when they occur, and in the moment of awareness, choose to participate or not and also be aware of the cost of your choice.

Sometimes the downward spiral is less obvious. It can be sneaky. It often sounds very intelligent, well thought out and rational. It can even sound polite and funny. So I am going to give you an effective tool to help you identify the downward spiral so you can quickly and easily identify it.

Look out for the three C's—criticism, complaining and condemnation (judgment)—and avoid them. The three C's are the hallmarks of the downward spiral. Benjamin Franklin once said: "Any fool can criticize, condemn and complain, and most fools do."

Imagine what it would be like if your work environment were free of the three C's. What would it be like for you to be there every day if there were no downward spiral? It would probably be blissful, productive and efficient. Practice awareness of the downward spiral and build muscle to stop it in its tracks!

If you practice identifying the downward spiral, you will be able to quickly see it for what it is and stop it—or at least not add fuel to it.

Stop the Downward Spiral

You can recognize and then stop the downward spiral in three ways:

1. *Realize:* Practice identifying the downward spiral quickly and early on. See it for what it is and don't be fooled!
2. *Refrain:* When you don't add fuel by participating, the downward spiral will dissipate. Step away—or don't join in— and just keep silent.
3. *Redirect:* Change the direction of the conversation by asking a question such as:
   - What do you want to have happen?
   - Where do you want to go from here?
   - What are you committed to?

Be bold enough to become known as the person who doesn't tolerate downward-spiral thinking and speaking. After all, you have trained people to know your threshold for the downward spiral. Now you can set a new standard. But do so with compassion, respect and kindness. Don't use this new awareness to judge others. That's just another downward spiral.

Think and Speak Possibility

According to motivational speaker and author Benjamin Zander, the passageway "out of the downward spiral is to think and speak possibility." Possibility thinking and speaking is positive in nature, and it always moves things forward powerfully. It includes communication that is kind, respectful, truthful and, above all, clear and steeped in integrity.

When we think and speak possibility, decision-making is easier, we more effectively influence others and we accomplish tasks more efficiently and creatively. We tell the truth. When we are in a state of possibility, our eyes are shining and we are enthused, excited, motivated, passionate and productive. We are open to new ideas and approaches, and we welcome creative thinking and innovation—we are engaged!

Nonverbal Communication

Impeccable communication depends not only on how powerfully we speak but on how well we manage our body language and tone. Becoming a masterful communicator requires us to be mindful of and responsible for what we are projecting all the time and the effect we have on others.

James is a tall, lanky engineer. When seated in a meeting, he tends to slouch and fold his arms. Because his innate tendency is to be somewhat reserved, he typically avoids direct eye contact, preferring to keep his focus on his notepad. When asked how they interpret James's body language in meetings, his colleagues remarked that they thought that he was disinterested in their opinions, which made them feel inferior. They therefore tended to withhold their opinions and just agree with him. That's good for James, because he gets his way, but bad for the company because valuable input from the team was sacrificed. When confronted with the issue of his body language, James was embarrassed. He explained that none of his colleague's assumptions were accurate. In fact, the reason he was slouched with his arms folded, he said, was because the meeting room was very cold.

Research shows that our communication is conveyed primarily through our body language (55 percent), our tone (38 percent) and the words we use (just 7 percent).

Body language expert Patti Wood wrote in her book *Success Signals* that our nonverbal communication consists of how we use space, touch, movement, gestures, objects, time, sounds and more:

"Our body language 'vocabulary' is made up of more than 700,000 different physical cues, including gestures, posture, movement, touch and more than 20,000 possible facial expressions. Nonverbal communication includes all communication that doesn't make use of words and also takes into consideration such factors as territory, appearance, scent, accessories or artifacts, even room design, color and time use."

Apparently, even the way you shake someone's hand says volumes about you and your relationship to that person.

Some tips to remember about using body language to communicate with integrity:

- A firm (but not hard) handshake helps you to establish rapport.
- Use eye contact to convey that you are fully present while another person is speaking to you, but don't stare at the person in an intimidating manner.
- Keep your posture straight and your shoulders back to convey alertness and enthusiasm and to help you stay alert and enthusiastic.
- Let your smile be a real smile, from your chin to your eyebrows.

You Are in Control

To help you think and speak possibility more consistently, ask yourself the following questions about what you intend to say—before you say it:

- Is it kind and respectful?
- Is it necessary? (Will it move things forward powerfully?)
- Is it the truth? (Or is it my opinion?)

When you ask yourself these questions, you will notice that the quality and integrity of your speaking improves.

A Communication Success Story

One of our Alliance consultants delivered an Excellence program to the office personnel of a small company that could best be described as dysfunctional. The staff never had meetings. Employees didn't talk to each other. They were suspicious of each other, and generally disengaged. For the most part, people came to work and just did what they had to do, convinced that they were undervalued, misunderstood and disrespected. Our consultant was naturally concerned that the program she had just presented was a disaster and that participants hadn't gained anything at all from the training. She was sure that they would just go back to their old habits and that nothing would change.

Two weeks later the company held its annual conference for staff and clients. To everyone's surprise, the conference was a big success. Customers reported that the service they received at the event was far superior to the service they had received in the past. Feedback was extremely positive. In his keynote speech, the president of the company acknowledged for the first time that the success of the company was dependent on the quality of its relationships, both external and internal, and that he was committed to extraordinary customer service. This was a major breakthrough!

Upon returning to the company several weeks later for a follow-up results meeting, the consultant discovered the Excellence program had in fact been the instrument of major change. Employees were now cooperating and collaborating. It was clear that communication had improved dramatically and that the work environment had improved, as had productivity. Staff were even having fun!

Practical Steps to Improve Communication in Your Company

- *Establish a "three C-free zone:"* The three C's—criticism, complaint and condemnation—are the hallmarks of unproductive communication. When you disallow them, you create an environment of possibility.
- *Discourage gossip:* We live in a culture obsessed with gossip—such as who's next in line for layoff, who made a poor decision and who didn't deliver as promised. When you discourage people from gossiping in your office, you free up time to focus on what's really important.
- *Speak possibility:* Engage your people in thinking and speaking about what's possible. When the conversation isn't going anywhere, ask, "What do you want to see happen?"
- *Look for the good:* Human nature tends to focus on what's not working and how things went wrong. Make an effort to acknowledge and reward what is working. Ask questions such as:
  - Where are we succeeding?
  - What are we doing well?
- *Focus on wins:* Start and end every conversation (including meetings) with what's working, successes and accomplishments. Ask questions such as:
  - How did you excel this week?
  - How will you excel next week?
  - What are you most proud of this week?
- *Ask bold questions:* Making assumptions and taking things personally accounts for a good part of our workday. The best way to keep from making assump-

Action Plan Principle 1

Use Your Word Wisely
Commit to improving the quality of your communication:

→ Stop downward spiral thinking and speaking.

→ Avoid the three C's (criticism, complaint and condemnation).

→ Think and speak possibility.

→ Align your body language, tone and words.

→ Use every interaction as an opportunity to move things forward.

tions and taking things personally is to ask lots of questions. Instill in others the courage to ask bold questions until they fully understand the meaning of what is being said.

- *Make a weekly deposit:* Commit to leaving a personal note or voice mail for all of your team members at least once a week to inspire them to bring out more of the best in themselves.

Top 5 "Do" List

1. List every downward spiral conversation you think, speak, hear, enable and endorse in your work environment, whether it be via e-mail, in meetings, during third-party conversations or over lunch.

2. When you have identified these conversations, for one week, sharpen your awareness by putting a check mark next to the conversation every time you think, speak, hear, enable or endorse it.

3. At the end of the week, determine the total number of downward spiral conversations to which you have been exposed and identify the effect those conversations had on you. Did it affect your productivity, cause you to waste time, distract you or drain your energy? If so, what was the cost to you (e.g., results, success, sense of accomplishment)?

4. Now that you are more aware of the negative impact that the downward spiral has on you and your colleagues, make a new commitment to redirecting these conversations, as early on as you can, to what's possible, where you want to go from here and what you want to see happen. Track your success by putting a star next to every downward spiral conversation that you successfully redirect.

5. At the end of the week, determine the total number of conversations for possibility that you actively generated. What effect did they have on you, your colleagues and everyone in your environment (e.g., more positivity, increased energy, better focus)? How does this result help achieve better business results?

Insights and Commitments

1. What insights did you gain from these action items?

2. What is your commitment regarding communication as you move forward?

3. How will you hold yourself accountable? (What processes, strategies and support systems will you put in place to help you keep your commitment?)

2 Be Accountable

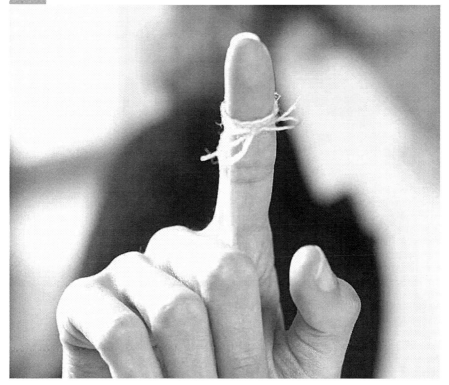

You are proactive and passionate,
even in tough circumstances.

chapter 6

Principle 2: Be Accountable

"People and organizations find themselves thinking and behaving 'Below the Line' whenever they consciously or unconsciously avoid accountability for individual or collective results. Stuck in what's called the victim cycle, they begin to lose their spirit and will, and eventually they feel completely powerless. Only by moving 'Above the Line' and climbing the steps to accountability can they become powerful again."

— Conners, Smith, Hickman
The Oz Principle: Getting Results Through Individual and Organizational Accountability

One day while waiting to pick my son up from school, I noticed a new banner on the school fence that said: "Excellence starts with you."

At first, my reaction was to think "how corny," and I plunged into criticism, complaint and condemnation about the school, faculty, staff and even the way parents double-park in the parking lot. After a while, I started to think about what the sign really meant. It dawned on me that Excellence does start with us (you and me). Ironically, many times, particularly in today's organizations, we have a tendency to sit and wait until the proverbial "they" take the first steps, until *they* take accountability and until *they* get the picture—and until *they* do, frankly, we have permission not to. After all, if *they* don't make a change, then how can we be expected to?

When I present the Excellence principles to groups, one of the most common questions is, "How can we be expected to excel when our leaders are such poor examples of excellence?" In other words, "Before we are willing to make changes, *they* have to. And, because they probably won't ever make the changes, there's no need for *us* to bother." This is quintessential "victim behavior."

Excellence requires courage and a willingness to step up, take risks, tell the truth and take action irrespective of what *they* (leadership, customers and team members) are doing or not doing. Excellence is about *us*, not them!

Be Accountable is a very powerful principle that offers you a new way of thinking about accountability. It also provides a practical model to use as you work to increase accountability in your organization. Accountability builds on and is inextricably linked with the first principle of Excellence: *Use Your Word Wisely*. Accountability demands wise use of our words, and conversely, wise use of our words requires a high level of accountability.

Accountability is a popular concept. We talk about it a lot, wonder what it takes to be accountable and shake our heads in bewilderment when we notice others are not being accountable. But, I wonder to what extent we fully grasp what accountability is, and if we are fully competent in identifying it, addressing it and instilling it in others and ourselves.

Are you effective at identifying lack of accountability in others? How about in yourself? Have you mastered the ability to effectively address nonaccountability with others? Do you consistently act at the highest level of accountability, no matter how tough the circumstance?

I like the description of accountability in the book *The Oz Principle:* "Accountability is an attitude of continually asking 'what else can I do to rise above my circumstances and achieve the results I desire?' It is a proactive perspective that focuses on current and future efforts as opposed to a reactive perspective that focuses on historical explanations and excuses."

Accountability is Not Blame

John was a senior operations officer at a successful software solutions company. He was a firm believer in accountability. The problem was that his interpretation of accountability was synonymous with blame. He instituted a process of assigning names to every task in a project plan, not a bad practice in itself—in fact, one that was already used on a regular basis to ensure everyone knew who was doing what.

John's process broke down, however, whenever there was a problem. Rather than using the task list as a way of pulling all the involved parties together to determine

Excellent Strategy

Michael Minsberg, president of Creative Lighting, rewards people by paying attention to their needs and interests. He makes it a point to read the sports page every Monday so he can discuss the highlights with staff who are sports enthusiasts.

the root cause of the problem and resolve it, the task list became a means of identifying who messed up. John would call a meeting of the project team, and instead of facilitating a solutions-oriented discussion, he would resort to name-calling, table-pounding and threats delivered in a shrill yell. The result? Telling the truth stopped. Collaboration shut down. People began to search for a suitable excuse that would shift the blame to someone else. In short, under the guise of holding people accountable, John effectively destroyed teamwork and possibility thinking.

Over time, because John didn't see the change he desired, his behavior became even more aggressive. He would interrupt work sessions to which he had not been invited, demand to see the agenda and make accusations that the team was "hiding something" or "not telling the truth." He discussed employees and teams with other employees. When this practice was challenged, he said that "healthy competition" kept everyone "sharp." He began to give duplicate assignments to different work teams to pit them against one another.

Poor John—he mistakenly thought that if he micromanaged and bullied his employees, they would become more accountable. In reality, his behavior had the exact opposite effect. In the climate of mistrust, the team members began to protect themselves and jockeyed for John's approval by blaming one another. Meetings became painful exercises in futility as the attendees either made excuses or refused to speak altogether. There was no collaboration or partnering to reach workable solutions; the teams were hopelessly locked in the downward-spiral conversation. The attrition rate soared as employees tired of the constant negativity and work disruption.

How accountable are people in your organization? Do your employees focus on the future and how they can rise above their circumstances to produce extraordinary results, despite the risk? Or do they tend to focus on old explanations and excuses, react to problems and fail to take full responsibility for the way things are?

Accountability requires integrity. When people are accountable, they acknowledge what's not working and are willing to assume ownership. They work proactively and cooperatively to resolve the situation. On the other hand, when they are not accountable, they tend to point fingers and blame others for the way things are. They fail to speak out truthfully, and they protect themselves—generally waiting for someone else to do something about the problem. The cost of nonaccountability can be crippling. It can cost your organization its spirit and power. To "lock in" accountability, you must implement systems that encourage risk-taking, truth-telling and having the courage to make mistakes.

One strategy you can use to help you hold yourself more accountable is asking the question, "What can I do?" instead of asking, "Why did this happen to me?" John G. Miller wrote in his book *QBQ! The Question Behind the Question:* "Questions that contain an 'I' turn our focus away from other people and circumstances and put it back on ourselves, where it can do the most good."

Begin to Accept Responsibility

Maggie called me six months after participating in the Excellence program to tell me she had finally "got" the principle Be Accountable and shared a wonderful story. You might be thinking it strange that it took her six months to understand the principle. Sometimes it can take a while for a principle to really sink in. Here is her story:

One morning, late for a very important meeting, Maggie realized her gas tank was empty. She rushed to the gas station, inserted her card at the pump and noticed the LCD display said "Sorry, can't read your card." Her stress level was rising rapidly, and Maggie inserted the card again. The LCD display again said, "Sorry, can't read your card." By this time, Maggie was very irritated. She tried once more, selecting the "credit" option instead of the "debit" option. Sometimes that works better. Again, her card was rejected. By this time, she was infuriated and ready to yell at someone. She marched into the convenience store, approached the young man behind the register and let him have it. When she had finished her tirade, the cashier asked to see her card. She slapped it down on the counter. The cashier picked it up, examined it carefully and said, "Madam, you are using your driver's license."

When things are not turning out the way we would like or expect, it is easy for us to look outside of ourselves for the reason. How often do we, in a stressful or demanding situation, fail to ask ourselves what we can do to rise above our circumstances? What we tend to do is point fingers, assign blame and expect someone else to take responsibility for the way things are.

Figure 6-1:

New Ground Rules for Accountability

- We recognize when we are not being accountable and take steps to be more accountable.
- We avoid ignoring and denying problems, or placing blame on others for the way things are.
- We actively "own" problems, and we then strive to solve and act on them in the best possible way.
- We behave proactively, focusing on what's possible rather than on explanations and excuses.

I am not suggesting that we all need to be like Gandhi or Mother Teresa, but the question is what would be possible in our organizations if everyone, regardless of title or position, were passionate, committed and operated at the highest level of accountability?

One of the popular slang phrases in today's lexicon is "my bad!" While slang may not be appropriate for your circumstances, it's a refreshing example of people admitting they made a mistake. The next step, of course, is to rectify the mistake and take steps to make sure it doesn't happen again.

In order for us to understand accountability better, we are going to identify how we think, what we do and say when we are being accountable and when we are not being accountable.

The Courage to Be Accountable

Accountability is not static. It fluctuates as you move back and forth between the behaviors. Sometimes you move quickly into accountability, and sometimes you can get stuck for long periods of time in nonaccountability. The goal is early detection and the discipline to move back into the realm of accountability as quickly and efficiently as possible.

When we face tasks that are difficult, challenging or uncomfortable, we tend to be less accountable. It's easy to be accountable for what's easy and enjoyable. Sometimes, we fall into the trap of thinking accountability is taking the initiative and responsibility for pointing out who is not being accountable. That's not the case.

Being truly accountable and accepting responsibility means that we must engage in the following actions:

- Be conscious and see things as they really are.
- Avoid finger-pointing, blaming and denial.

Activity Accountability

In your *Excellence Journal*, answer the following questions:

What do people think, say and do when they are not being accountable?

_____

_____

_____

What are the signs of nonaccountability?

_____

_____

_____

Next, define accountable behaviors and attitudes.

_____

_____

_____

What do people think, say and do when they are being accountable?

_____

_____

_____

What are the signs of accountability?

_____

_____

_____

What needs to be in place (systems, processes and ground rules) for accountability to exist in your organization?

_____

_____

Activity Accountability (cont.)

Identify one difficult situation your team is currently facing and answer the following questions:

How accountable are you being?

_____

_____

_____

_____

How is this your level of accountability affecting your success?

_____

_____

_____

_____

What would be the reward or payoff for being more accountable?

_____

_____

_____

_____

What actions would you need to take to be more accountable?

_____

_____

_____

_____

- Refuse to sit around and wait for someone else to fix the problem.
- Take ownership of the problem.
- Resolve the situation fully.
- Take accountable action.

David, a customer service manager, was intrigued by a conversation we were having about accountability. Grappling with the concept, he posed the following question to his group of fellow managers: "If the phone were ringing in the reception area and you noticed the receptionist wasn't there to answer, what would you do?" Lots of ideas emerged, from ignoring the phone since it wasn't their responsibility to sending an e-mail to the receptionist's manager to inform her of the problem. After much discussion, I suggested that the highest level of accountability would be to answer the phone, address the customer's inquiry and then immediately tell the receptionist's manager directly about the issue so that the matter was fully resolved. My suggestion caused an uproar in the group as they emphatically informed me it was not their job to take care of a ringing telephone. Eventually we agreed that, bottom line, this was their company and they were responsible for everything that takes place in the building. This is a very unusual perspective, particularly in larger companies in which roles and responsibilities become blurred, and people tend to operate in "silos" or isolation.

An Accountability Success Story

Jill, a freelance writer, had been writing short interviews for a magazine for about a year. Usually, the editor e-mailed her new assignments each month, and Jill performed the interviews and got them to the editor by deadline. But early in the second year, the editor decided to send Jill a list of all the upcoming assignments for several months in one e-mail. Jill relegated the e-mail to the backburner and wound up missing her deadlines. When the editor called, demanding to know where the missing articles were, Jill was caught off guard and initially began hemming and hawing and acting as if she didn't even know about the articles. But she had been through training in Excellence and had studied the principles. She immediately remembered what she'd learned and then took full responsibility for the failure to meet the deadline. "I will get these done today and will make sure this doesn't happen again. It's entirely my fault," she said. She did get the interviews done that day, and the editor quickly forgave her lapse.

Practical Steps to Increase Accountability
- *Encourage Risk:* Encourage risk by asking, "If you assumed 100-percent owner-

Action Plan Principle 2

Be Accountable
Commit to increasing accountability:

→ Gain awareness of your accountability strengths and challenges.

→ Illuminate your accountability "blind spots" by asking others to point out situations in which you could be more accountable.

→ Take action to increase accountability in every area.

→ Stop making excuses.

ship, what would you do?" Hold "Risk Forums" in which employees present opportunities to try a new approach or to do something differently. Actively acknowledge and reward people for taking risk.

• *Celebrate Failure:* When people feel comfortable failing, they will be more likely to assume higher levels of accountability. Make failure okay in your organization by speaking about it openly and using it as a learning opportunity. Ask your people to report on their failures. When someone or something fails, say, "Hmmm, how interesting! What can we learn from this?"

• *Hold Accountability Forums:* From time to time, gather your team for an "Accountability Forum." Use this forum to inventory opportunities for exercising increased accountability. Ask questions such as:

- What kinds of excuses are we making?
- How could we be more proactive?
- If we took total responsibility, what might we do differently?

• *Identify Accountability Blind Spots:* Sometimes it's difficult for us to see when we are not being fully accountable. Seek regular feedback from everyone your group interacts with to illuminate "blind spots." Ask, "Where do you see opportunities for us to be more proactive?"

• *Request the Truth:* More than ever, we must have the courage to say what we mean and mean what we say, even when others don't like it. Expect and request the absolute truth from everyone. Acknowledge and reward the truth.

• *Don't Tolerate Victims:* "Victim" behavior is the cause of low spirit, lack of discipline and poor results. When you encounter "victim" behavior, ask, "What would you need to do to feel more powerful and effective in this situation?"

Top 6 "Do" List

1. Identify one situation in which you are denying there is a breakdown, blaming others, pointing fingers or waiting for someone else to do something to fix the situation, or identify a situation in which you are just worrying and feeling hopeless, frustrated, resigned or powerless.

2. List all the excuses you are making to "let yourself off the hook" that give you permission not to take action to resolve the situation powerfully and proactively. (Example: "It's not my job," "I've tried a million times before and failed" or "I don't have time.")

3. What are these excuses "costing" you? (What negative impact do they have?)

4. List all the actions you would need to take in order to proactively resolve the situation. Begin with committing to stop making excuses and instead add actions (e.g., be proactive, fully own the situation and be 100-percent responsible).

5. How would you benefit if you were to take the actions you listed?

6. Now take the actions you listed. Be confident and powerful, as if you knew you couldn't fail.

Insights and Commitments

1. What insights did you gain from these action items?

2. What is your commitment regarding accountability as you move forward?

3. How will you hold yourself accountable? (What processes, strategies and support systems will you put in place to help you keep your commitment?)

3 Focus

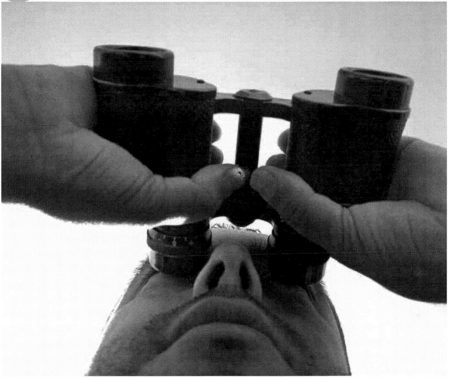

You align your daily actions and behaviors with what matters most.

chapter 7

Principle 3: Focus

"The individual who wants to reach the top in business must appreciate the might of the force of habit—and must understand that practices are what create habits. He must be quick to break those habits that can break him—and hasten to adopt those practices that will become the habits that help him achieve the success he desires."

—J. Paul Getty

We are all faced with extraordinary demands. We want more from others and ourselves, and others need more from us. We want to be the best we can possibly be. The reality is that we feel too busy to take the time to take inventory, to align with what really matters and to search for more meaning in our lives.

Who has the time to pursue deeper purpose? Mostly we are on autopilot, flying through the day meeting as many obligations as we can without questioning and then reaching for more. The result is that we are working long, hard hours, but at the end of the day we lack a sense of accomplishment.

Nancy, a director of IT, had worked for her company for more than 10 years. She was respected by her peers and her employees, earned a good salary, enjoyed matching 401(k) contributions and had good job security. To many people, that kind of life might sound enviable. But Nancy was miserable. "I was killing myself to stay on top of my workload," she said. "My team was under constant pressure to produce results in a chaotic environment filled with changing priorities and shifting goals. It was physically draining. I would literally work night and day, and I got nowhere," explained Nancy.

"Most of my day was spent putting out fires, trying to buffer my staff from the barrage of IT requests and responding to unreasonable demands from management." A year later, Nancy decided to leave and went to work for a company that offered a better match for her values.

To what degree are you and your team focused on what really matters? Do you consistently execute on priorities (personal and organizational) and achieve a sense of satisfaction and fulfillment? Or is your attention fragmented as you frantically run through the day putting out fires, which leaves you fatigued and frustrated?

When our daily actions and behaviors are aligned with our deepest values and grandest vision, we experience a sense of meaning and well-being. When every person on your team is aligned with what is really important and is guided by the same core values, it creates a powerful surge of energy and sense of pride.

Focus is a very powerful principle that will give you a new way of allocating your time and energy, one that brings you the deepest sense of satisfaction and fulfillment. This principle builds on and is inextricably linked with the first two principles of Excellence. Wise use of our words and accountability require focus, and focus requires a high level of accountability and impeccable use of our words.

When an aircraft flies from one point to another, most of the time it will stray off course. The role of the pilot or autopilot is to constantly bring it back on course. The same ideas apply to Excellence. Most of the time we might find ourselves being pulled off course by old habits, patterns, routines and systems. So we need to establish new structures (a new autopilot system) to keep bringing us back on course.

Intention and Attention

Focus is a function of intention and attention. Intention is knowing what is important to us and being committed to that no matter what. Attention is consistently attending to that which matters most. This may sound simple, but it takes discipline to consistently act on what is really important to you. For example, how many times have you said that holding regular one-on-one meetings with your staff is important, but then canceled or postponed these meetings due to conflicting priorities? For many managers, their intention to develop a strong, connected relationship with employees is not supported by their habits.

Be Present

Focus also means being present, giving people your full attention. How often do you find yourself talking to someone while you are downloading e-mail or performing some other task and therefore diluting your effectiveness? We all know

---

Figure 7-1:

New Ground Rules for Improved Focus

- We understand that excellence is a function of focus.
- We adopt new behaviors and practices that help us achieve excellence.
- We focus on what really matters to the organization, the team and each individual.
- We align our daily actions with organizational and personal values so that we experience fulfillment.
- We set aside a few minutes every day to plan the best use of our time and energy.
- At the top of every hour, we ask ourselves, "How can we extract the greatest value from our efforts?"

---

that people's most basic need is to be seen and heard, and yet we live in a world in which multitasking is expected. We thus neglect to give people our full attention and often leave them feeling unacknowledged and invalidated.

Among the tribes of northern Natal in South Africa, people greet each other with the expression "sawu bona" instead of the traditional "hello." The expression "sawu bona" means "I see you." If you are a member of the tribe, you might respond by saying, "sikhomna," which means "I am here." When we genuinely "see" people and truly connect with them by really asking and really listening, even if only for a brief moment, we validate them and inspire their trust and respect.

Mike, a salesman with Rustoleum, had a problem. One of his customers was an older man who liked to tell stories. This customer took valuable time out of Mike's day and threw off Mike's sales schedule. While he was a steady customer, he was not one of Mike's best. Mike began to dread calling on him. Finally, he came up with the brilliant idea of putting this customer at the end of the day so the long-winded gentleman wouldn't ruin his schedule. Mike realized that his customer needed somebody to hear him, he needed somebody to listen to his stories.

"I realized I could give him that while I was getting what I needed without impacting my bottom line," Mike said. The customer felt appreciated by Mike, and Mike was able not only to keep a valued customer but also to do something kind for another person. He was able to focus on the customer and be fully present to him instead of worrying about his next appointment.

Ask yourself, "How can I improve the quality of my presence with others?" It may be as simple as just turning off your blackberry, cell phone or telephone when talking with others.

Where Are We Going?

The two most important questions employees have are "Where am I going?" and "How am I doing?" Answering these questions regularly is important for maintaining clarity and focus. Clear organizational, departmental and team goals allow individuals to understand how their contributions add value—and their engagement, accountability and performance all increase.

A technology division of American Express was able to cascade goals from a senior vice president to the 800 people in the division. The end result: The costs of developing a software system were cut in half over a two-year period.

Focusing has many facets. The most important is being in alignment with your own personal goals and values so that you find meaning and fulfillment in what you do. Knowing what really matters to you and aligning your daily actions and behaviors with what matters is the path to Excellence.

Do You Have Purpose?

A few years ago, the city of Miami embarked on a highway beautification project that included planting trees. Whenever high winds came up, the trees were blown over, and city workers were dispatched at great expense to prop the trees back up with external supports. This happened over and over again. For some reason, the city hadn't realized that in a high-wind area, the trees needed a deeper root structure.

The same phenomenon can play out in our lives. When we lack deep roots (e.g., firm beliefs, compelling values that we live by), we are easily buffeted by the prevailing winds of stress, change, demand and uncertainty. When we lack a strong sense of purpose, we cannot hold our ground. When challenged, we tend to react defensively, blaming, disengaging and ceasing to invest energy.

Purpose is a source of energy and power. It fuels our direction, gives us focus, passion and perseverance. What is your purpose?

Identify Your Guiding Values

A successful organization must have a strong sense of purpose and direction—compelling values that are deeply integrated in the culture and driven by a shared commitment to the organization's vision and mission. We, too, must have such a sense of purpose and direction.

If we are going to develop a strong sense of purpose and direction that can help us withstand the demands we face, we need to know what really matters to us and what our guiding values are. Then we need to align our daily actions and behaviors with these values so that at the end of each day we feel like we accomplished something that really matters.

Activity Goals

What is your organization's direction?

_____

_____

_____

What are the primary business goals?

_____

_____

_____

What are your core values?

_____

_____

_____

Identify your team or departmental goals and show how they are linked to organizational goals. Talk with every member of your team about how his or her individual goals fit into the big picture.

_____

_____

_____

_____

_____

_____

_____

_____

Alignment Saves Energy

When the tires on your car are not in alignment, the ride is rougher and you tend to veer off course more easily. (You also get lower gas mileage.) You have to tightly hold on to the steering wheel.

To what degree are your daily actions and behaviors aligned with what matters most

Activity Identify

In your *Excellence Journal*, answer the questions and complete the sentence so you can identify what matters most to you. Later in this chapter, you will use this activity to develop your personal purpose statement, which will help to give you a strong sense of direction.

1. What word best describes you?

2. What trait do you want to pass on to your children?

3. Life, liberty and the pursuit of …

4. What are two rules everyone should follow?

5. What word best describes the person you most admire?

to you? If you look back over the past week or month or year and audit everything you said and did, to what degree would your actions and behaviors be a true reflection of what you say is really important to you?

Activity Identify (cont.)

6. What is your greatest strength?

_____

_____

7. What single thing are you most proud of?

_____

_____

8. What would you like to be known for in your organization?

_____

_____

9. If you couldn't fail, what one thing would you like to accomplish at work?

_____

_____

10. As you look back, what one thing would you change or do differently at work?

_____

_____

11. What is the one Excellence principle you are committed to mastering?

_____

_____

_____

_____

_____

_____

When you are in complete alignment, you feel more positive, energized, motivated and fulfilled. You experience a deeper sense of integrity and fulfillment. This translates into improved productivity. When you are out of alignment, you feel frustration, lack of accomplishment, emptiness, inability to be present, fatigue, stress and burnout. Your productivity becomes compromised.

If you were committed to living your life with the deepest integrity, what adjustments or changes would you need to make in your day-to-day life to accomplish that?

As a leader, why would it be valuable for you to discover what really matters to the people who work with and for you? Differences in guiding values can be valuable if they are honored and harnessed, or they can be a source of friction if they are not understood and harmonized. They can affect decision-making, collaboration and systems. The most powerful way to motivate people is to value what matters to them and use that to inspire them.

Develop a Purpose Statement

Values are our mirror—they keep us on course and renew us when we wander off course. The most effective way to leverage our commitment to our values is to convert them into a purpose statement (or a personal vision statement) that is a declaration of our purpose/direction/commitment in life.

Your purpose statement identifies what you want to accomplish, how you want to contribute, what you want to be known for and what you want people to say about you. It is a declaration of who you are and what you are committed to in life. It should express the value you want to offer, the things you would like to accomplish and the kind of person you want to be known as. It is a proclamation of what matters most to you.

Your purpose statement is bigger than you are, and it cannot be accomplished next week. It is big and bold in a way that calls you forward to excel, and it seeks to extract more of your unrealized potential and make you challenge yourself.

Begin crafting your purpose statement using your responses in the previous activity. Phrase your statement in the present tense, not the future tense, beginning with "I." Creating your statement may not be an easy or quick process. You might choose to work on it for several days—or even weeks. Use the following guidelines:

- I am … (combine your answers to questions 1-8 in the previous activity)
- I am committed to … (your answers from questions 9 -10 in the previous activity)
- I can be counted on to … (your answer from question 11 in the previous activity).

Know what you want, know why you want it.
Discover your talents, use them daily.
Work hard, work smart.
Give unconditionally, love unconditionally.
Find your purpose, live your purpose.

—Jack Canfield et al., *The Power of Focus*

When you have a working draft of your statement, say it out loud to someone you trust and watch for a reaction. If the response is positive, you are on track. If, on the other hand, there is no reaction, go back and revise your statement.

When you are finished, post it in a place where you and others will see it every day. Review it every morning to get yourself on track. Share it with others so they will help to hold you accountable for what you are committed to. Use it as a tool to help you make better decisions about how you allocate your time and energy each day. Also, use it to help you maintain balance in your life. Refer to it when you need to recalibrate yourself and clarify your direction.

Implement New Habits

Your purpose statement and topmost values can be a very powerful tool for you to use to sharpen your focus and improve your effectiveness.

Brian Tracy is a master author, consultant and trainer on personal achievement. In research he conducted, he found that people who spent 15 to 20 minutes a day first thing in the morning planning their day experienced a 26-percent increase in effectiveness in the period of one year. The morning planning included a review of their major goals, a restatement of their commitment to those goals and a plan for the best use of their time and energy for that day. Other Tracy studies have found that people who actively set goals are in the top 3 percent of the population.

I invite you for the next 30 days to set aside a few minutes first thing every morning to review your purpose statement and ask yourself the following questions:

"How can I best align my time and energy with what matters to me?"

"How can I extract the most value from my efforts and produce the best results while achieving the most satisfaction?"

Action Plan Principle 3: Focus

Focus
Commit to improving your focus:

→ Set aside a few minutes at the start of every day to plan what's most important.

→ Look for ways to extract the greatest value from your efforts.

→ Align your daily actions and behaviors with your organization's goals, your department's goals and your personal goals.

→ Be present to others.

When you are true to your commitments, you live a better, more productive, more fulfilling life!

Do you think it would be worthwhile trying this? What kinds of results might you expect?

A Focus Success Story

In his book *Silos, Politics and Turf Wars: A Leadership Fable About Destroying the Barriers That Turn Colleagues Into Competitors*, Patrick M. Lencioni describes the term "silos" in corporate culture as "a metaphor drawn from the large grain silos that one sees throughout the U.S. Midwest. It is a term of derision that suggests that each department on an organizational chart is a silo and that it stands alone, not interacting with any of the other departmental silos."

Toy giant Mattel was an example of discord and inefficiencies due to a silo culture that resulted in a sometimes contentious and aggressive culture. Disconnected corporate silos at Mattel blocked the flow of information and undermined important workforce strategies.

"The culture could be contentious and aggressive at times. How well you did could depend on how poorly somebody else did," said Alan Kaye, senior vice president of human resources, according to a June 2006 article in *Workforce Management* magazine.

The article goes on to show how Mattel got back on a healthy footing, in part due to a massive employee-development initiative. CEO Robert Eckert began by creating a corporate strategy and a vision that would give the individual business units a common objective.

"Employees within the silos knew what they were individually trying to accomplish, but they had no clue of where Mattel was headed as an organization," Eckert is quoted as saying. An awareness-raising campaign outlining corporate goals was directed toward

Excellent Strategy

Recognition of Excellent behaviors at HR Solutions is simple but meaningful. When an employee witnesses a co-worker being excellent, he or she gives that person a beautiful lapel ribbon with an inscription of the behavior being rewarded.

Mattel employees around the world. Kaye, however, did not want workers to merely recite the corporate strategy. Because corporate philosophies are often abstract, he wanted the employees to visualize their roles within the organization and to deepen their understanding of how the business functions.

Kaye and his team in human resources designed "learning maps" that depict some of the critical functions within Mattel. The diagram illustrates how the different departments—such as global marketing, design and concept, market research, engineering and promotion—contribute to the company's process. The maps also show how each department's work contributes to the overall health of the organization.

According to Mattel's leadership, the change in focus helped Mattel's internal promotions increase by 25 percent during the preceding five years. Leadership noted that nearly three-quarters of open positions are now filled internally. In the same time period, turnover among nonmanufacturing personnel decreased by 50 percent. Annual attrition rates are now 7 percent to 8 percent.

Practical Steps to Improve Focus:

- *Get in Alignment:* On a regular basis, review the five topmost organizational values. Then ask each employee to identify his or her own five topmost values. Discuss where organizational and personal values are aligned and where they are not. Any disparity between organizational and personal values can be a major source of discontentment.
- *Pass the Photo:* Pass photos of your employees around the table. Ask each person to select one photo and answer the following questions:
  - What is important to this person?
  - How can I help him or her be more successful?
  - What does this person need from me to bring out more of the best in himself or herself?
- *Ask Them What Really Matters:* Get inside the heads and hearts of your people. Ask them:
  - What really matters to you?

- What are your grandest goals?

Then do whatever you can to support them in achieving those goals.

- *Perform Periodic Tune-Ups:* Ensure your people are maximizing their time and focus by asking the following questions:
  - Are you making the best use of your time and energy?
  - Which tasks might you minimize or bypass?
  - How can you apply more of your best?
- *Eliminate Drains:* The work environment is full of distractions and energy drains. Identify all the factors that interfere with the ability to focus and then work to eliminate them (e.g., poor lighting, background noise, disturbances).
- *Be Present:* When someone wants to talk to you, either tell them, "This is not a good time," or turn off your computer, pager and phone so you can focus fully on the conversation. Give your full attention.

Top 4 "Do" List

This week you will fine-tune your planning and sharpen your focus by following these four steps:

1. At the start of the week (ideally on Sunday evening, or very first thing on Monday morning), complete the following planning exercise:
   - Write down your five topmost values.
   - Now enter at least one action item for each day of the week directly on your calendar that will ensure you perform actions based on your five topmost values. For example, if one of your topmost values is "family," then one action item would be to have a family dinner on one day of the week. The goal is to make a commitment to your personal values before you commit to anything else.
   - Then review your list of things to do for the week, including all work-related projects and any other necessary tasks. Prioritize them based on their urgency and their importance to accomplishing your organization, department or team goals. Be sure to include any personal tasks you want to accomplish. Allocate your time in a way that will extract the greatest value from your efforts.

2. First thing in the morning, every morning, set aside 10 minutes to review your five topmost values and your personal vision statement. Plan what's most important. Make a commitment to yourself that everything you do and say each day will be a reflection of what really matters to you.

3. Be 100-percent present to whatever is in front of you. If you are working on a

project, ask to not be interrupted so you can concentrate fully on the task. If you are in a meeting, be fully engaged. If you are talking with someone, give him or her all of your attention. Wherever you are, be there completely. Plan to be nowhere else!

4. At the end of each day, every day, set aside 10 minutes to review your day.
   - How well did you use your time and energy?
   - Did you accomplish those things that matter to you most personally (spend time with family, exercise, act with integrity, etc.)?
   - Did you focus on tasks that are most important to the fulfillment of your organization's and department's goals?
   - Do you end the day with a feeling of accomplishment and a sense of pride and satisfaction? If not, what do you need to do differently tomorrow? Go to sleep knowing you did your very best. Promise to begin tomorrow with passion and focus.

Insights and Commitments

1. What insights did you gain from these action items?
2. What is your commitment regarding focus as you move forward?
3. How will you hold yourself accountable? (What processes, strategies and support systems will you put in place to help you keep your commitment?)

4 Mine The Gold

You bring out the best in yourself and others.

chapter 8

Principle 4: Mine the Gold

"If you're not thinking all the time about making every person more valuable, you don't have a chance. What's the alternative? Wasted minds? Uninvolved people? A labor force that's angry or bored? That doesn't make sense! If you've got a better way, show me. I'd love to know what it is."
—Jack Welch, former CEO of General Electric

The nature of gold mining is very challenging. The work conditions are often deadly—dark, dank, a lack of oxygen and dangerous. The reward is significant. The job of the miner is to relentlessly hack away at the rock to find the nugget of gold. Your job as a leader is the same. In the worst conditions (and sometimes those that seem hopeless and are frustrating), your job is to relentlessly mine the gold in others. As long as other people work with or for you, or use your product or service, the only way you will be successful with them is to consistently relate to them from the point of view of their unseen potential and recognizing their hidden or forgotten value.

Mine the Gold changes the way in which you relate to others and gives you the opportunity to improve collaboration, increase cooperation and bring more harmony to your interpersonal relationships. You are able to more easily influence people to achieve the desired result.

Sometimes *Mine the Gold* sounds elementary, so we brush it off because we think we have already mastered it. Most of us grew up with mothers, fathers, grandmothers, grandfathers or teachers who taught us to be kind and considerate of others and to treat them as we would have them treat us. I believe we intend to live like that. But there is a deeper level to this idea that we may be overlooking. Doing so may compromise our ability to get the best from others.

Unleashing Potential

My colleague Shannon said that when she is with me she feels that she needs to be her best. I never told her she has to be. But as I hold myself to a higher standard of conduct, she feels the need to do so also. She is on top of her game when she is with me. I want to be able to have that influence on everyone.

In its most basic form, *Mine the Gold* means we believe in others. That is, we affirm their worth, trust they want to be their best and mindfully relate to them with respect and kindness. I don't think anyone wakes up in the morning and says, "Today my commitment is to be as doggoned awful and unproductive as possible."

But *Mine the Gold* goes one level deeper than that. The principle suggests that excellence is about researching and understanding where people have unrealized potential, and then, in the most artful way, seeking to unleash that potential so that they bring more of their talent, skill, knowledge and creativity to the table every day.

Think of someone you have worked with (or for) who, for the most part, didn't pay much attention to you and who was uninterested in your success. That person ignored your accomplishments, overlooked your opinions and suggestions. Without explicitly saying so, that person concluded that you weren't going anywhere (except out the back door) and that nothing you contributed was going to change his or her mind. How did you respond in that situation? You probably felt resigned, apathetic, victimized and frustrated. Perhaps you gave up trying and just did enough to get your job done.

Now think of someone in your life (a teacher, mentor, boss or coach) who consistently believed in you, never gave up on you, always encouraged you to excel, authentically praised and acknowledged your accomplishments, stimulated you to expand and grow and found ways to extract more of your talent and skill. How did you respond in that situation? You were likely motivated, enthusiastic and passionate. I suspect you tried harder, worked more and were extremely loyal to that person.

Maximize Success—Theirs and Yours

The more we mine the gold in others, the more loyal, creative and productive they are. The more we create opportunities for success and maximize the success of others, the more they want to give. And the more success they experience, the more successful we are.

We live in a corporate world in which sometimes we get caught up in our own

Figure 8-1:

New Ground Rules for Improved Relationships

- We treat others as they can and should be treated, knowing they will become as they can and should be.
- We are always asking ourselves how we can bring out more of the best in ourselves and others.
- We are constantly expanding our definition of excellence, knowing that yesterday's definition is no longer valid.
- We create a work environment based on community, non-competitiveness and joy.

greatness. We protect ourselves, our reputations and our jobs, but we forget that serving others and helping them to succeed is what makes us truly successful.

To mine the gold, we must be able to see the gold, focus on it and extract more of it. It sounds logical, yet our working relationships often break down and are fraught with tension and conflict.

The Treasure Chest

The Treasure Chest is a metaphor for the talent, skill, creativity and good we all have inside of us. Over time, our beliefs, judgments, opinions and criticism about others accumulate and make it difficult for us to see and relate to the "gold" in them. The Treasure Chest becomes shrouded in negativity.

Why? Well, human nature tends to analyze and judge. This is good, because it often protects us from danger, but at the same time it can cause our relationships to atrophy and deteriorate.

Imagine that you have worked with Ralph for a few years. Right from the start, you had a problem with his inability to deliver work on time. You tried to let it go, but the next time you worked together on a project, he did the same thing. You later find out that others in your organization have had similar experiences. Now you have a whole group of people who agree with you and validate your belief that Ralph is unreliable. You now have the expectation that he will always be unreliable. In fact, you are so sure of this that you may even circumvent Ralph and plan around him, or just do things yourself rather than ask him to help. You are so certain that he is unreliable that there is practically nothing he can do to make you see things differently. In some way, Ralph realizes that you have labeled him and that he cannot succeed in gaining your approval. He disengages, and you stop bothering to try to extract the value he may offer.

In your Excellence Journal, write down the name of a person you work with

Activity Relationships

In your *Excellence Journal*, list all of your relationships that over time have become clogged—relationships that are uncooperative, uncollaborative or just characterized by underlying tension. Include relationships with your direct manager, peers, direct reports, other teams and departments. Include every relationship you would like to improve.

_____

_____

_____

_____

_____

_____

_____

_____

Next, identify at least one action you will take to begin restoring the relationship and what the reward for taking that action might be. Then perform that action.

_____

_____

_____

_____

_____

_____

_____

_____

_____

whose name is synonymous with irritation. Now write down all the judgments and beliefs you have accumulated about that person. If you were to wipe the slate clean and start fresh with this person, how would that be valuable?

The Clogged Drain

As our relationships deteriorate, it is as if the drains have become clogged. Think of how when you wash your hair in the shower, after a few weeks or months, the drain becomes clogged with hair, and the flow of water is slowed down. Similarly, as our relationships become clogged by built-up judgments, it becomes increasingly difficult to interact with others, to make good decisions and to collaborate for the good of the company. Meetings thus become laborious, decision-making is hampered and gossip is rampant. All of these negative outcomes compromise our ability to excel. Gerry, a director of product development, commented, "It was a revelation to discover how many 'clogged drains' our executive team has, and the issues we need to address to effectively lead the organization."

Can you identify any clogged drains in your company? How do they affect the success of your business?

Road Kill

When we consistently neglect to bring out the best in others and find that the drains have become clogged, the result is road kill. What do I mean by that term? I mean that—like a small animal we may hit and kill while driving our car at night in the countryside—we can relegate someone to nonexistence as far as we are concerned. I'm talking about subtly and covertly blocking out people from our consciousness—dismissing them, excluding them, overlooking them and discounting them.

The existence of road kill can have disastrous effects. John, the CFO, and Bill, the director of sales, had never seen things the same way. Over the period of a year, their relationship had deteriorated to such an extent that it was the main topic of conversation in the company. In fact, many of the employees had become frustrated with the elaborate systems and additional measures they had been instructed to take in order to assist the two executives in circumventing each other. It had become a standing joke. Even the CEO just rolled his eyes when the topic came up. In the process of accommodating their inability to work together, the company invested a significant amount of time and resources. In addition, the credibility of the senior leaders had been severely compromised. When I spoke with the two men about the negative impact their situation had on the company,

Excellent Strategy

> **At the Pepsi Bottling Group San Diego division, managers look to catch drivers and merchandisers "in the act." When employees go the extra mile they receive a "caught in the act" card they can exchange for a prize.**

neither was willing to make any adjustments—both preferred to continue treating the other as road kill.

How can a company grow and succeed when two key executives refuse to communicate with each other? It can't, and this company did not grow. The communication breakdown caused sales to decline and profits to decrease, and the company limped along with a high rate of turnover and dissatisfaction.

Signs of Road Kill:

- We pretend not to see someone walk by.
- We roll our eyes when they say something stupid.
- We fold our arms and turn away from them.
- We don't return their calls or e-mails.
- We see their number on caller ID and let the call go to voicemail.
- We "forget" to include them in a meeting or decision.
- We ignore their opinions.
- We work "around them."

Giving an "A"

The way to deal with road kill is to give others an "A." This doesn't mean we literally give people an "A" or "exceeds expectations" on their annual performance review. Giving others an "A" is a metaphor representing a way of relating to others that inspires them to be their best. The environment of an "A" is one of joy, relief, ease, community and risk taking in which people are excited about the possibilities for them to exceed expectations.

Darrel is a well-respected customer support manager for a software company. He is known to be very effective at managing people, and his team consistently receives a 95-percent customer satisfaction rating. That's something every manager wants. After participating in a classroom learning session about giving an "A," Darrel decided to give it a try. At his regular weekly staff meeting, instead of focusing on the errors, weaknesses and areas for improvement, he concentrated on giving his staff an "A." He began the meeting by asking his team how he could leverage their talents. At first, they were suspicious and asked what new management book he had read. But he was persistent in his explanation that in order for the team to overcome the challenges presented by a software release plagued by bugs, he would need to capitalize on their strengths and look for ways for each of them to add more value. His employees were excited, and they initiated a dialogue for discovering ways in which they could capitalize on their strengths. The adjustment Darrel made was minor but very powerful.

Giving an "A" can be as subtle as responding to people's calls, including them, looking them in the eye when talking to them, asking for their opinions and treating them with respect. It's a subtle shift in the way we relate to them that imperceptibly allows them feel different around us. They feel that they have the opportunity to succeed in new ways.

Benjamin Zander uses this technique to great effect. In his book, *The Art of Possibility*, Zander relates the story of how he learned the valuable lesson of giving an "A." He was teaching a class at New England Conservatory when he realized that the students were in such a state of anxiety over the grades they would receive that much of his material was lost on them. They were not performing to their full potential. He and his wife Rosalind decided that they would give each student an "A" for the course, with the condition that the student write a letter detailing "the story of what will have happened to you by next May that is in line with this extraordinary grade." The results were extraordinary. The students set their expectations high and met them. They were not distracted by the anxiety of receiving a good grade. They were invited as full participants into the teaching and learning process.

It is not in the context of measuring people's performance against standards that we propose giving the "A," despite the reference to measurement the grade itself implies. We give the "A" to lessen the judgmental power that grades have over our consciousness from our earliest days.

Practical Steps for Mining the Gold
- *Acknowledge Successes:* Begin and end every meeting with an acknowledgment of successes. Ask questions such as:
  - What would you like to be acknowledged for?
  - How did you excel this week?
  - How will you excel next week?
- *Mine for Unrealized Skills and Talent:* There is often a wealth of unrealized skill and

Action Plan Principle 4

Mine the Gold
Commit to improving your interpersonal relationships:

→ Mine the gold in others by recognizing, affirming and relating to them from the point of view of their unrealized potential.

→ Seek ways to extract more of people's skill, talent, creativity, loyalty and brilliance so that they experience more success.

→ Give others an "A" by creating an environment of joy, relief, ease, community and opportunity.

talent in organizations. To tap into these hidden resources, ask questions such as:

- What are you good at that I don't know about?
- What job other than the one you are in now would you choose and why?

- *Let Glory Emerge:* Each month, nominate an employee for "glory." Request that all other team members look for and acknowledge how this person contributed and excelled.

- *Make Them Visible:* Look for every opportunity to promote the accomplishments of your team to the rest of the organization. Consider having a success-related bulletin board, hosting an accomplishment breakfast or publishing a newsletter that highlights your team's successes.

- *Make Recognition a Habit, Not an Event:* List all of your employees. Each month, place a check mark next to each person's name when you have authentically recognized him or her for something exceptional. Keep looking!

- *Treat Them Like Gold:* When it is a job seeker's market, will your employees choose to stay with your organization, or will they go elsewhere? Employees who are treated with respect, given opportunities to grow and encouraged to establish meaningful relationships at work are more likely to be loyal. When you treat your people like gold, they will not only stay but will also be willing to consistently do their best.

Top 5 "Do" List

1. Identify a person whose name is synonymous with irritation and/or frustration. The person should be someone with whom you have difficulty collaborating and cooperating.
2. List every good thing you can think of about the person who irritates and/or frustrates you. Write down all of his or her skills, talents, accomplishments and value. Mine for the gold!
3. If you were to be compassionate and forgiving, and "wipe the slate clean" with this person, that is, if you were willing to give up your preconceived ideas and not be "right," and instead focus on his or her strengths and value, how would that benefit you and the other person?
4. Now, make a commitment to give the person an "A" this week. Look for opportunities to acknowledge the person by affirming and reinforcing his or her value. Be kind and be positive to show your genuine interest.
5. List five things you can do or say this week to bring out the best in the person and then do them!

Insights and Commitments

1. What insights did you gain from these action items?
2. What is your commitment regarding relationships as you move forward?
3. How will you hold yourself accountable? (What processes, strategies and support systems will you put in place to help you keep your commitment?)

5 Strive For Balance

You are vital and energetic as a result of a balanced life.

chapter 9

Principle 5: Strive for Balance

"I commend to you the simple practice of spending one hour a day, every day, sharpening the saw physically, spiritually, and mentally. This is called Daily Private Victory. It will affect every decision, every relationship. It will greatly improve the quality, the effectiveness, of every other hour of the day, including the depth and restfulness of your sleep. It will build the long-term physical, spiritual, and mental strength to enable you to handle difficult challenges in life."

—Stephen Covey
The 7 Habits of Highly Effective People

Jerry is an endodontist who has no idea how to relax. For years he has done nothing but work. Even when he's at home, he is busy doing chores or taking care of paperwork. He has a family, but they have learned to function without him. Financially, he is a success and can pay his employees well, but he has a difficult time keeping staff in his office. He expects them to work through their lunches and to stay late regularly, even though he does not pay them extra. In his practice, he could schedule patients for two visits to accomplish what needs to be done, but he refuses to do so and continues working on a patient long after his staff should have gone home. His entire office staff has turned over five times in the past six years. He thinks that because he has no reason to leave work, his staff should be content not to have a life outside of work as well. His appointment taker has now stopped booking as many patients, and referring dentists are getting upset because of that, which may make it difficult for him to sell his practice. Jerry is getting older but is terrified at the prospect of retirement because he has not built any kind of life outside of his work.

Nancy is a top manager at a television network. She is in charge of a staff of between 15 and 20 people. Like Jerry, Nancy has not created a healthy work-life balance. If employees don't leave town for their vacations, she expects them to come to meetings. In her view, weekends are for working. Because of Nancy's overzealous work ethic, the television network has lost top talent, and Nancy has become isolated as her supervisors try to find a spot for her where she will not cause even more people to leave. Nancy is a prime example of someone who works harder but not smarter.

Do these scenarios sound familiar? The names have been changed, but both of the situations come from real life. You have probably met people like Jerry and Nancy, or you may even have some of their habits and expectations yourself. Excellence at work means knowing when to put work aside and give attention to other aspects of your life. It may be as simple as reading a book, taking a walk or doing something else that you enjoy.

Excellent leaders make a conscious effort to bring balance into their lives.

"Sharpening the Saw"

There is an old story about Sven the Lumberjack. Sven had just started a new job, his best job ever. For each tree Sven chopped down, he would be paid a good sum of money. He set his goal for the first day to chop down 100 trees.

The first day he worked hard and cut down 100 trees. He decided to set his goal for the second day even higher, at 110 trees. The second day he worked very hard and chopped down 110 trees. He set his goal for the third day to cut down 120 trees. On the third day, he worked extra hard and extra long until evening. Eventually, he dragged himself home having only cut down 90 trees. He could not understand how, despite working harder and longer, and despite his intense focus and motivation, his performance was suffering. Feeling frustrated, he approached his supervisor, asking for advice.

The supervisor listened to his story and then asked, "Did you stop to sharpen your saw?" You see, he had been so busy chopping and sawing, he had forgotten to make sure his tools were in peak condition. So it is with us. We are so busy chopping and sawing and expecting increasingly more from ourselves and others that we forget to stop to sharpen our tools, to take inventory and to reassess, refocus, realign and renew ourselves.

In his book *The 7 Habits of Highly Effective People*, Stephen Covey reminded us to "sharpen the saw." Unfortunately, in a corporate world where taking time for recovery and renewal is often frowned upon, and where the leaders in our organizations typically associate time to rejuvenate with laziness, it is even more difficult to attend to our health and well-being. The result is that we work excessively and think we are increasing productivity when in fact we often become less and less effective.

The demands of our work, family and life, along with the changes, stress and uncertainty of the world we live in, all take a toll on our organizations and on us. Unfortunately, this toll is invisible to us until it becomes a serious problem. We often wait until we get sick before we take time off to relax.

To exist in a state of excellence, we must be able to sustain a high level of well-being. Well-being is a function of self-management—constant balancing and rebalancing—as well as a function of taking adequate time for recovery and renewal. Renewal in all areas of our lives is important. We all know of people who have success in one area of their lives but are weak in other areas. When we neglect one area of our life, the others tend to be negatively affected as well.

The two last Excellence principles, *Strive for Balance* and *Lighten Up*, focus on vitality, energy and well-being, which are critical components of excellence. To perform at peak levels, we must have consistent physical, mental, emotional and spiritual energy.

What is the level of energy and vitality in your organization? Are people able to sustain a high level of energy and vitality over a prolonged period, bringing passion, excitement and enthusiasm to the workday? Or are they fatigued, stressed and burned out due to poor life balance?

Strive for Balance provides the fuel for excellence. No matter how well we have mastered the other Excellence principles and no matter how committed we are to personal mastery, we cannot sustain excellence in the absence of energy and vitality. I have never come across a highly successful person who dragged herself around slouching, sniffing and being negative. Excellence inevitably comes with an expression of liveliness, enthusiasm, passion, energy and vibrancy.

In their book *The Power of Full Engagement*, Jim Loehr and Tony Schwartz tell us that the most important organizational resource is energy. If energy (physical, mental, emotional and spiritual) is depleted, the reservoir of potential energy in the organization is low, and when there are demands, stress or change present, the organization lacks the resources to meet the challenge.

Work-life effectiveness strategies go beyond individual responsibility for balance. As part of a Total Rewards program, you should institute specific organizational

Figure 9-1:

New Ground Rules for Balance

- We eat healthy, nutritious foods, exercise regularly, get enough rest and effectively manage our stress.
- We are engaged in continuous learning, always seeking ways to expand our mental capacity.
- We have a deep sense of fulfillment and peace of mind, because our daily habits are a true reflection of what really matters.
- We sustain healthy, supportive relationships at work and at home.
- We seek renewal and replenishment through appropriate spiritual practice.

practices, policies and programs to promote a healthy work-life balance for everyone in your company. These policies and programs can include any programs that help employees do their jobs effectively, such as flexible scheduling, telecommuting and child-care programs.

There are seven major categories of organizational support for work-life effectiveness in the workplace that address the key intersections of the worker, his or her family, the community and the workplace. The seven major categories are:

- Workplace flexibility
- Paid and unpaid time off
- Health and well-being
- Caring for dependents
- Financial support
- Community involvement
- Management involvement/culture change interventions.

A philosophy that actively supports efforts to help employees achieve success at both work and home, such as that embodied by the Excellence principles, will be embraced by workers. When embedded into the corporate culture, such a philosophy will create healthier and more satisfied employees and leaders.

A Model for Balance

The following is a model for balance that can help you gain new insights about creating and sustaining improved balance and thus increased energy and well-being. This model presupposes that there are five primary dimensions or areas in our life that form the foundation for our health and well-being: physical, intellectual (mental), emotional, relational and spiritual.

Physical:

Our physical strength is the foundation for our overall health and well-being. It is the fundamental source of fuel for life. When you are physically in balance, you do the following:

- Eat healthy, nutritious food that strengthens you and creates vitality.
- Drink plenty of water.
- Get enough rest and relaxation.
- Effectively manage stress.
- Get regular physical exercise.

Intellectual (Mental):

Our intellectual health provides us stimulation and expands our cognitive capacity. We are either growing intellectually or we are decaying. When you are mentally in balance, you do the following:

- Seek varied sources of mental stimulation.
- Continue to learn, not only in your field but in many different areas.
- Participate in personal and professional growth opportunities.
- Read vigorously and on varied topics.
- Insist on associating with others who are positive and who stimulate your thinking.

Emotional:

Our emotional health enables us to withstand stress and change. Optimal emotional health yields positivity and an overall feeling of satisfaction in life. When you are in emotional balance, you do the following:

- Feel secure.
- Have a high level of self-confidence.
- Have strong feelings of self-worth, believing you are making a valuable and relevant contribution to the world.
- Effectively manage your emotions and sustain a positive outlook.
- Experience a high level of congruence between your daily actions and behaviors, on the one hand, and your five topmost values.

Relational:

Our relationships can be a significant source of strength or a drain on our energy. When your relationships are in balance, the following is true:

- Your relationships are secure and healthy.

Excellent Strategy

When an employee at Encore Capital Group wants to recognize a co-worker, he or she awards him or her with a "values block" from a set of plastic Lego-type blocks imprinted with the company's values: integrity, respect, fairness, collaboration and breakthrough results.

- Your relationships are fulfilling.
- Your relationships are nurturing and adequately nurtured.
- You have a strong sense of community and support at work.

Spiritual:

Our spiritual health is our core, our center and our commitment to the value system we choose. Some people find spiritual fulfillment in prayer, meditation, reading or being outdoors. It's where we get our renewal and strength; it's our opportunity to recalibrate. Staying spiritually healthy is why a personal mission statement is so important. When we have a deep understanding of our purpose, we can review and recommit to it. When you are in balance spiritually, you do the following:

- Regularly seek spiritual renewal.
- Set aside time to recalibrate.
- Understand and review your purpose on a regular basis.

The first step in achieving better balance is to identify patterns of imbalance—areas/dimensions that are weaker than others. Second, revisit what really matters to you by reviewing your five topmost values and rebalancing by aligning your daily actions and behaviors with what matters most to you (i.e., apportioning your time and attention first to what matters most and then to all the other matters).

Sometimes this means you have to reassess your commitments and make adjustments. Perhaps you need to let go of or delegate things that are not urgent and important so you can free up enough time and energy to take care of your well-being (the things that really matter to you). By letting go of things that are not essential to your well-being, you can then make other commitments that are consistent with your core values, your vision and your wildly important strategic goals (personal, professional, individual and organizational).

A Balance Success Story

When it came time for the employees at Modern Postcard, a company you'll learn more about in Chapter 17, to assess their effectiveness at maintaining balance, many of them realized that they were not doing very well. Most people thought of balance only in terms of work-life balance until I suggested they look at all aspects of their lives, including the physical, intellectual, emotional and spiritual. But Steve Hoffman, the CEO and owner of the company, was different. He had achieved optimal balance by attending to all areas of his life. This was eye-opening for members of his staff. They realized that he was constantly reading books, working out and nurturing his relationships—while at the same time effectively and energetically running the company. Steve served as an inspiration to his employees about how to balance their own lives. They realized an important secret to his success and began to be more interested in finding ways to create more balance for themselves.

Practical Steps to Improve Balance

- *Role Model Balance:* When you role model a healthy, balanced life, your staff will imitate you. When you successfully marshal and sustain physical stamina, mental clarity, emotional connectedness and spiritual alignment, you will communicate the importance of balance and establish the same expectation for others.
- *Take an Energy Poll:* When you ask, "What is your energy level?", you create an expectation for high energy. When the answer to the question is "low," ask, "How might you increase your energy?" Then provide encouragement and support.
- *Manage the Energy:* Eating strategically ensures a steady supply of energy. Remove sugary, high-fat, energy-draining snacks from your workplace. Provide a supply of healthy, high-protein, energy-giving foods such as fresh fruit, energy bars, nuts and lean turkey slices.
- *Encourage Them to Drink:* Drinking water is important for good health. Remove caffeinated drinks such as coffee and sodas, which provide temporary spikes of energy but cause dehydration and fatigue. Instead, offer pitchers of fresh iced water with lemon. Encourage employees to drink at least 64 ounces (or eight glasses) of water each day.
- *Walk & Talk:* Use one-on-one meeting time to take a walk outdoors. You make the same time investment, have the same or better quality of conversation and increase your physical energy.

Action Plan Principle 5

Strive for Balance
Commit to achieving greater balance in your life:

→ Identify areas of your life in which you are not operating at optimal effectiveness.

→ Clarify what really matters to you and take steps to achieve balance in the areas of your life.

→ Make new commitments to effectively manage all areas of your life.

→ Spend one hour a day, every day, sharpening your saw.

- *Allow Time for Recovery:* Balancing stress and recovery is essential to sustained performance. Recovery helps prevent burnout and stimulates creativity. Encourage your employees to pace themselves, allow them time for plenty of breaks and let them know it's OK to close their eyes and rest for a few minutes.

Top 3 "Do" List

This week, commit to spending one hour a day, every day, improving the quality of your physical, intellectual, emotional, relational and spiritual health. Your goal is to take time for renewal and create a reserve of energy.

1. Identify the areas of your life that most need attention. Rank them in order of importance by writing a number between 1 and 5 next to each one (1 is most important and 5 is least important).

    ___ Physical (eating habits, exercise, stress)

    ___ Intellectual (mental stimulation, learning, discovery)

    ___ Emotional (feelings of self-worth, confidence)

    ___ Relational (relationships with family, friends, co-workers)

    ___ Spiritual (feelings of connectedness, purpose)

2. Identify one new commitment you want to make in each of the areas you've identified as important. What new outcome or result do you want to produce in each area? (Example: I am committed to working out regularly to achieve a strong, lean body.)

3. Now set aside one hour every day this week to focus on one of the commitments you just made.

Insights and Commitments

1. What insights did you gain from these action items?
2. What is your commitment regarding balance as you move forward?
3. How will you hold yourself accountable? (What processes, strategies and support systems will you put in place to help you keep your commitment?)

6 Lighten Up

You remember not to take yourself so seriously.

chapter 10

Principle 6: Lighten Up

"Humor and laughter are perhaps the best way we can 'get over ourselves.' Humor can bring us together around our inescapable foibles, confusions, and miscommunications, and especially over the ways in which we find ourself acting entitled and demanding, or putting other people down, or flying at each other's throats."

—Rosamund Stone Zander and Benjamin Zander

The Art of Possibility: Transforming Professional and Personal Life

Did you know that studies show more than 1 million people are absent from work every day in the United States due to stress-related illnesses? According to the Stress Institute of America's latest figures, stress is costing U.S. employers about $300 billion per year in lost productivity, health-care and replacement costs.

In a study to test the impact of stress on people's immune systems and their ability to withstand illness, it was found that exposure to five minutes of something uplifting significantly increased people's immunity levels for up to six hours. On the other hand, when people were exposed to five minutes of stress, their immune systems were significantly lowered for up to six hours. What does this mean to your business? It means that when your employees are stressed, they are more susceptible to illness, and absenteeism increases, affecting your bottom-line results.

Do you have a fun, enjoyable work environment in which people thrive? When people bring lightheartedness, humor and fun to work, they enjoy their work more and thrive. Quite simply, they are more eager to get to work in the morning and do their very best. On the other hand, when the work environment is staid and serious, employees tend to lack energy, passion and enthusiasm. When we lighten up, we create a fun-filled, inspired workplace in which we naturally produce better results and feel more connected.

Lighten Up is the probably the most important Excellence principle, but often not the easiest. If we master the other principles but fail to derive joy from our work, excellence becomes a burden. The sixth principle says: Let's just not take this all so seriously. Let's have our desire and intention for excellence and masterful leadership give us energy, create vibrancy and stimulate us to be outrageous, charismatic and engaging risk-takers.

We tend to let our personal importance, or our ego, get in our own way, and we become afraid of what others will think and say. Therefore, we contain and restrict ourselves in order to behave in an appropriate and politically correct manner. While it is important in the workplace to be appropriate and respectful, we should not feel that we cannot enjoy ourselves and have fun.

If you're a parent, you've probably noticed just how seriously kids take their playtime. They love to play. They are passionate about it. And they are continually learning as they play. The challenge for us is to bring that same sense of play into our work. Let it be fun. Let there be laughter in the air. It doesn't mean that things aren't getting done.

I think we have forgotten that work is supposed to be fun—and that people produce even better results when they are enjoying themselves. To increase joy at work, simply intend to bring more lightness and humor to the day. Find ways to make other people's day more enjoyable. Create an environment of joy in simple ways.

How Humor Helps

At the beginning of the chapter, I reported a statistic about the effects of stress-related illness on absenteeism in the workplace. Laughter is a quick, safe, over-the-counter cure for stress. Laughter helps us relax and, according to some studies, actually boosts our immune system. You probably already know the story of how Norman Cousins cured himself of ankylosing spondylitis, a debilitating disease that doctors gave him little chance of surviving. Since then, scientists have confirmed a connection between mirthful (as opposed to malicious) laughter and health. According to researcher Dr. James Walsh, laughter is good for our bodies because it massages all the organs of the body. No wonder we feel better after we've had a good laugh.

Laughter has not only been shown to reduce stress and improve our health, some scientists have proven that it can affect the quality of our thought processes. Dr. William Fry, professor emeritus of psychiatry at Stanford University, points out that

Figure 10-1:

New Ground Rules to Lighten Up

- We remember not to take ourselves so seriously.
- We seek ways to bring fun and laughter to our work day.
- We allow time to relax and play.
- We look for opportunities to make other people feel good.

laughter improves our creative powers. "Creativity and humor are identical," he says. "They both involve bringing together two items which do not have an obvious connection, and creating a relationship."

Most people know by now that the left and right hemispheres of the brain are in charge of different aspects of brain functioning. Humor actually involves both hemispheres. Patti Wooten, a nurse and author of several articles and a book on humor and healing, cited research by Dr. Joseph Dunn and wrote the following:

Humor is a cognitive skill that uses both sides of the brain. The left side of the cerebral cortex is active during the telling of a joke, but as the humor is perceived (as we interpret what we hear as funny), the brain wave activity moves toward the right side of the cerebral cortex. Humor brings together the whole brain, linking the logical left brain with the creative right brain. Several research studies have shown that after perceiving something humorous, we become more creative at problem solving.

So we've seen that humor and laughter elevate physical health, creativity and whole-brain thinking, but what about the social benefits? If you're striving for an excellent organization, then you want everyone in that organization to feel as though they belong. Joseph Richman, M.D., professor emeritus of psychiatry at Albert Einstein Medical Center in the Bronx, New York, found that telling jokes heightens our sense of "belonging and social cohesion" and decreases "our feelings of alienation." Needless to say, if your workers feel a sense of belonging, then they are more likely to stay with your organization.

A perfect example in the business world is Southwest Airlines, which has built a culture on joy and merriment. Terrence E. Deal and M.K. Key, authors of *Corporate Celebration: Play, Purpose, and Profit at Work*, note that "Play pays." They wrote, "[T]hose who play together, stay together, and work together. Dividends are profitability plus an enlivened workforce. High levels of morale, commitment and a sense of purpose and camaraderie prevail when celebrations are frequent, focused, and authentic."

Deal and Key cite the following example: When Southwest Airlines's Nashville operation launched service to Orlando, Florida, the company turned its section of the

Action Plan Principle 6

Lighten Up
Commit to lightening up and enjoying work more:

→ Be charismatic and fun—don't take things quite so seriously.
→ Bring lightness and humor to work.
→ Look for ways to make other peoples' day more enjoyable.
→ Establish new rituals and practices to bring joy to your workplace.

terminal into a beach party. The staff dressed up in beachwear—straw hats, sunglasses— and painted their noses with zinc-oxide sunscreen. Passengers were given ripe oranges as boarding passes while calypso music played in the background. They even held a limbo contest to involve passengers in the fun.

Lighten Up Success Story

Earlier I related a story about a company that went through the Excellence program with one of my consultants. The small office was completely dysfunctional, and communication was marginal. After they went through the Excellence program, they began to lighten up. One of the "games" they began to incorporate at the beginning of meetings was "Translation." One person would tell a story in a completely made-up language, and another person would translate what the first person was saying. I think they got the idea from a television show. It only took a few minutes, but it gave the rest of the group a hearty belly laugh, relieved tension and energized the meeting.

Practical Steps to Lighten Up

* *Make Time to Have Fun:* As the leader, you set the tone of the work environment. When you allow yourself to loosen up, laugh and have fun, your people will too. Make a commitment to find five minutes each day to do something that promotes fun and laughter.
* *Make Someone's Day More Enjoyable:* At least once a month, identify one person on your team who will be "Employee of the Day." Ask the team to decorate this person's workspace and do something special to make his or her day more enjoyable.
* *Take an Attitude Poll:* When you walk into the office and greet others, rather than ordinary chit-chat or a "good morning" offered on the run, stop for a few seconds,

Excellent Strategy

Employees at the Welk Resort Group are immersed in the company's values and culture through a series of interactive board-game activities during their orientation. Teams compete and win prizes for providing the correct answers to questions about the company's history, safety guidelines and other standard operating procedures.

look people in the eye and ask them, "What is your attitude today?" Consider posting a daily attitude chart on which you write down your attitude at regular intervals during the day. Encourage others to participate.

- *Implement a Three O'Clock Rock:* In the middle of the afternoon, energy levels usually ebb and productivity diminishes. Implement a new ritual to refresh, renew and reinvigorate your people. Ask for volunteers to help initiate a quick three-o'clock interlude.

- *Play:* There are lots of ways to play that are appropriate to your work environment. Ask your people to come up with a list of ways to create a lighthearted environment. Assign each team member a day to create play activities.

- *Be Outrageous:* Let your desire and intention for excellence and masterful leadership give you energy, create vibrancy and stimulate you to be outrageous, charismatic and engaging. From time to time, let yourself go—do something unusual that will bring a smile to your employees' faces.

Top 3 "Do" List

This week, commit to lightening up by just not taking yourself and your needs so seriously. Make work enjoyable for yourself and others by finding ways to bring laughter and fun to your workplace.

1. List one thing you can do each day this week to bring more lightness and humor to work.

   Monday: _____

   Tuesday: _____

   Wednesday: _____

   Thursday: _____

   Friday: _____

2. Seek to make other people's day more enjoyable by doing something special to bring them joy. List the names of five co-workers whose day you would like to make happier. Allocate one day to each person on your list. Identify one action you will take to make his or her day more enjoyable.

    1. _____
    2. _____
    3. _____
    4. _____
    5. _____

3. Dialogue with your co-workers about establishing one new "ritual" that will help increase joy in your workplace.

Insights and Commitments

1. What insights did you gain from these action items?
2. What is your commitment regarding creating a fun work environment as you move forward?
3. How will you hold yourself accountable? (What processes, strategies and support systems will you put in place to help you keep your commitment?)

chapter 11

Review of Key Strategies

Ellen was scheduled to have a very difficult meeting with the president and CEO of her company. He was on a witch hunt. A recent employee survey included some very negative feedback, and he was meeting with managers to find out who said what, who were his enemies and who was on his side.

Ellen had no idea what to do to prepare for this meeting. She didn't want to get drawn into the negativity, the gossip, the "he said, she said." She didn't want to blame others for problems that the CEO had caused himself.

First, she decided to practice role-playing the meeting with a coach. When the time came for her meeting with the CEO, she was ready. Whenever he tried to get her to say something negative, she would respond in one of the following ways:

"I don't know. What do you think?"

"You could be right, but what are you really thinking here?"

"What would you like to see happen?"

She almost took on the role of an interviewer, or a counselor. By the end of the meeting, she hadn't told him anything. She hadn't lied or compromised herself either. When he was done, the CEO shook Ellen's hand and said, "This is the best meeting we ever had."

Ellen utilized several Excellence principles in this interaction. She refused to get caught up in the downward spiral. She was accountable in that she did not look for anyone else to blame for any problems. And she was mining the gold with her CEO by helping him to focus on ways in which he could be more effective.

The Strategies

In Part Two, we have focused on the Excellence principles, offering definitions, examples and methods for incorporating them into the workplace. This chapter will review strategies for each principle and offer clear and practical tools for bringing them into your life and work.

Use Your Word Wisely

Mastering the power of your words is simple, but not easy! Here are a few strategies:

- Stop the downward spiral—for yourself and for others. Do so with respect and kindness.
- Think and speak possibility. Use your words to inspire, give energy and convey the truth.
- Manage all your communication all the time. Align your body language and tone with your words for maximum power and effectiveness.
- Think of every interaction as an opportunity to move things forward to get extraordinary results.

Be Accountable

- Become aware of your accountability strengths and challenges. Take a hard look at your behaviors in all areas of your work life. Ask others for feedback to illuminate your blind spots. It is often much easier for others to identify situations in which you could be more accountable. So ask them!
- Take action. When you have identified a situation in which you could be more accountable, take action to be more accountable.
- Begin dialoguing with members of your group (team/department/organization) about how you can increase accountability. Ask questions such as:
  - How do we define accountability?
  - What are the ground rules for accountability in our group?
  - What systems are in place to support and encourage accountability?
  - Is accountability rewarded? How?
  - How do we address nonaccountable behaviors and attitudes?

Focus

- Set aside a few minutes at the start of every day to get your eye on the ball.
- Role model focusing in ways you never have before: be present to others.
- Share your purpose statement.
- Begin a dialogue with your group about what really matters—to the organization and to the individuals. Get in alignment.

Mine the Gold
- Gain awareness of your beliefs.
- Be bold and courageous in your forgiveness and compassion for other people, and be willing to start with a clean slate.
- Practice mining the gold in simple, authentic ways by giving others an "A."
- Remember to keep giving yourself an "A" too!

Strive for Balance
- Take care of your physical health by eating healthy foods (vegetables, lean meats, whole grains), drinking plenty of water and exercising moderately.
- Expand your mental capacity through continued learning.
- Engage in a spiritual practice that helps you find peace and replenishment.
- Remember to take time for friends and/or family.

Lighten Up
- Learn how to play again.
- Remember some funny stories from your life. Share them with others.
- Start off your next meeting with a clip from a funny movie you saw recently.
- Pretend you're David Letterman and make a top 10 list about your workplace.

How Fascinating!

And, when you fail at these strategies, don't judge yourself and make yourself wrong. Acknowledge your lack of excellence, forgive yourself and move on, with a commitment to doing better next time. Benjamin Zander in his book *The Art of Possibility* suggests a valuable way of regaining your perspective. Just throw your hands up in the air and, with great enthusiasm, shout out "How fascinating!" The point here is to recognize that you are human and not to take yourself so seriously.

Congratulations

Now that you have completed the activities for each of the
Six Principles of Excellence, you have developed a new set of
habits to last a lifetime. You have given your best and
achieved a new level of excellence!

How have the Excellence principles affected you, your work
and your life?

_____

_____

_____

_____

_____

What will you accomplish as a result of your new commitment
to excellence?

_____

_____

_____

_____

_____

_____

_____

_____

_____

_____

_____

_____

part 3

The Strategies of the Game

chapter 12

Become an Employer of Choice

Megan is a successful manufacturing engineer in her thirties. The first few months of her new job were exciting and stimulating. She was inspired by her manager's commitment to improvement and felt sure she would be able to contribute at higher levels than she had at her previous company. Most importantly, she was excited and confident the processes she was hired to implement would help her new company grow.

Over a period of a few months, I started to notice a change in her attitude. She began complaining about her boss's lack of direction, conflicting agendas of top leadership, the prevalence of gossip in her work team and an overall compromise of integrity in the company. Her health declined, she had difficultly sleeping and she admitted she was feeling depressed about her life. After several months, she finally acknowledged that she hated her job and was planning on looking for a new position. She said, "It's ironic that I am working for a high-profile company, earning a six-figure income, and all I can think about is leaving. The lack of integrity and accountability in my work environment is depleting me. My boss's lack of direction and support makes it almost impossible for me to achieve my goals. I hate going to work every day." Within weeks Megan found a better position at a *Fortune* 500 company.

Megan's story is symbolic of the changing workplace. Faced with abundant opportunities, young, talented professionals will no longer put up with a poor employment experience. Today's employees expect leaders to provide strong direction and inspire trust and respect. They are more demanding of their employment experience, more discerning of the work environment and less willing to work for a weak manager.

Today's labor market is a candidate-driven market. The telling evidence is the number of workers who are delivering the take-this-job-and-shove-it speech and leaving for a more rewarding, less spirit-crushing work experience. According to the U.S. Bureau of Labor Statistics's so-called quit rate, the number of people who have quit jobs has increased by a third since 2003. There are now about 2.6 million people leaving their jobs each month, the same level as in the pre-9/11 economy. (Business 2.0, May 3, 2006)

As competition for top talent increases, the only solution is to become an employer of choice.

Better Employment Brand Equals Better Performance

Your company's brand—the service or product you are known for, which attracts customers and drives financial performance—will become increasingly dependent on your "employment brand," the reputation your company has for the experience employees can expect. You can probably think of companies you know by their reputation as great places to work or terrible places to work. And while you may do business with a place that has a bad reputation, given the choice, you're more likely to do business with a company that you know has satisfied, happy employees—especially if you intend to do repeat business with them.

Your employment (or talent) brand is the key to attracting great talent and sustaining an excellent consumer brand. But, because brands are "states of mind," they are difficult to build and sustain, especially for companies not yet well established or for companies wanting to reverse some unflattering publicity. A strong employment brand places a compelling image of what it's like to work for your company in the minds of your target employee pool and energizes those people to apply for jobs in your company. It also develops a common theme among your employees so that they consistently speak of your company as a great place to work and encourage their talented and successful friends to seek positions with your company.

Genevieve, a Generation X manager, approached me after a presentation to thank me for inspiring her. As she had listened to my talk about the importance of becoming an employer of choice and offering employees a great work experience, she had realized the company she works for is not a great place to work. She was inspired to start seeking a new position with another company. Then she asked me a question I will not forget, a question that I believe will become increasingly common: "Can you recommend any companies that are truly employers of choice that I should consider working for?" I thought this was a smart question and an enlightened approach to job seeking. More importantly, it is indicative of a shift from an employer-driven market to a candidate-driven market. Employees are now becoming consumers of the employment experience, and are—and will continue to be—very selective about whom they choose to work for.

Google is an excellent example of a company with a strong employment brand. One gets a compelling image of what it's like to work for the company by viewing the career page on the Google Web site. In effect, Google has determined the DNA of successful employees and has a clear vision of the kinds of people it wishes to attract. In its description of what it's like to work for Google, the company expertly appeals to exactly those kinds of candidates:

At Google, our strategy is simple: we hire great people and encourage them to make their dreams a reality. We believe in hard work, a fun atmosphere, and the sort of creativity that only comes about when talented people from diverse backgrounds approach problems from varying perspectives. Googlers have been Olympic athletes and Jeopardy champions; professional chefs and independent filmmakers. We think you'll find Google a place where you can aspire to outsized accomplishments. There's still so much for us to dream and do.

As you identify your employment brand, you will want to focus on what is unique about the employment experience your company offers. Why should candidates choose your company? What is in it for them? Now that you will have to compete for top talent, you will have to market to them, just like you market to your customers. In fact, your employees are your new customers.

Strong Employment Brand Offers Competitive Advantage

Today's consumers are more conscious of how and where they spend their dollars, preferring to do business with companies that exhibit social consciousness—beginning with treating their employees well. This consumer attitude translates into a financial advantage for company leaders who create a positive employment brand. In their book *Built to Last: Successful Habits of Visionary Companies*, Jim Collins and Jerry I. Porras showed that companies that consistently focused on building a strong corporate culture over a period of several decades outperformed companies that did not by a factor of six and outperformed the general stock market by a factor of 15.

There's more evidence showing better performance by companies that strive for a culture of excellence. In an article titled, "Cultural Capital: The New Frontier of Competitive Advantage; Increasing Market Value by Leveraging the Intangibles," Richard Barrett wrote:

In 1998 there were 164 publicly traded companies represented in three lists of "best" companies: *Fortune* magazine's list of "100 Best Companies to Work For," *Industry Week*'s "100 Best Managed Companies" and *Working Mother*'s list of "100 Best Companies." Of these 164, 38 were on more than one list. These "best" 38 showed consistently superior financial performance over a 10-year period of several percentage points over the 164, and the 164 showed a consistently superior financial performance of several percentage points over the Standard & Poor's 500.

But this was not simply a one-time occurrence. Barrett also noted that, "During the 1990s the average annual shareholder return of the companies that make up the 100 Best Companies to Work For in America was 23%." This is 9 percentage points higher than the annual shareholder return of the Russell 3000 index (a general index of American industry).

That kind of financial performance appeals to investors. A hypothetical study conducted by the Russell Co. showed a portfolio of stocks from the companies that were on the first *Fortune* 100 Best Companies to Work For list in 1997. The study compared the overall financial results through 2003 of that portfolio with a portfolio of stocks from the Standard & Poor's (S&P) 500. The results were astonishing. Money invested in the "100 Best" portfolio would have returned almost three times more than the same amount as a portfolio in the S&P 500 during the past six years. The results were even more remarkable if, instead of holding on to the stocks of the 100 best companies, an investor had changed the portfolio to reflect the changes in the list annually. (Every year, a new list of the 100 Best is published in the Great Place to Work Institute's annual survey. Typically, about 20 companies are replaced.) If investors updated their portfolio with each year's 100 Best list, they would have seen the original investment outperform a comparable S&P 500 portfolio by more than a factor of five.

The Path to Building an Excellent Workplace

You can't declare your company an employer of choice, but you can declare the goal of being an employer of choice. Gaining recognition and earning the reputation as an employer of choice goes far beyond a few initiatives that make your company look good. It requires an integrated, metrics-based, long-term strategy that aligns all of your company initiatives. And even when you have earned a reputation for being a top employer, maintaining that reputation is quite another story.

Stacy tells the story of her application and interview process with a company that claims it is an employer of choice. The company had received recognition for workplace excellence and was touted as a great place to work. Stacy was excited at the prospect of interviewing for a position with the company and was duly impressed with the rigorous interview process. As is typical, at the end of a series of interviews with key decision makers, she was told someone would be in touch with her soon to let her know if she was hired. More than a month passed, and

Stacy didn't hear a word. She eventually called to ask if she was still being considered for the job. To her surprise, she was told the search had been called off and the position was not going to be filled.

Here's what Stacy said about the experience: "The reason I applied for a job at this company was because I believed it was committed to treating people with respect and maintaining a high level of integrity. The selection process was very poorly handled. I was treated rudely and with disrespect. It's obvious that this company does not back up its recognition as an employer of choice with action."

Becoming a sustainable employer-of-choice organization requires attention to every detail and every aspect of how you conduct business. Candidates are consumers of the employment experience, and they are most astute. Every little thing every person in your company says or does creates your reputation, and even a seemingly small oversight such as forgetting to inform a candidate that the company called off the search can have significant impact on your reputation as a great place to work. Unfortunately for the company Stacy interviewed with, accounts like this spread quickly in our highly connected world, and I suspect there are other talented people like Stacy who will choose not to work for that company.

Sometimes financial success can mask an unhealthy corporate culture. Brian, a CFO for a mortgage company, was pleased with his company's financial success, but realized that the corporate culture was unhealthy. Gossip was rife, insults and rude behavior had become acceptable and turf wars were becoming increasingly common. Brian realized that these bad habits and low standards of behavior were a primary cause of unusually high turnover, difficulty attracting good talent and mediocre performance, which in turn was affecting the quality of customer service. While the company continued to grow and show financial gains, the culture issues had been ignored. When business slowed, the CEO issued a directive to senior management to "clean things up" and help the company recover. Brian understood that the only way to grow the business through increased sales and revenue was to build a strong, vibrant workplace so that it could attract and retain great talent. He realized the pathway to that goal was to become an employer of choice. What he needed was a blueprint, a plan to achieve his goal.

The Excellent Workplace Model offers a practical step-by-step approach to becoming a sustainable employer-of-choice organization. Just like the Jenga game we played as children in which we built towers out of blocks, the elements of this model are interdependent and must be aligned with all other elements to ensure its sustainability.

Figure 12-1:

Excellent Workplace Model™

Create Value

Align Processes

Enlighten Leadership

Develop Excellent Managers

Establish a Culture of Excellence

Step One: Establish a Culture of Excellence

Culture is a magnet. A strong culture is the foundation of your employer-of-choice efforts. Culture is embedded in every aspect of your organization. It is like your company's operating system. Culture is the combination of attitudes, language and behaviors that pervades every aspect of your company. It guides how employees think, act and feel. It either attracts or repels top talent, and either alienates or bonds current employees. Whether it is positive or negative, your culture endures. The behavior that is modeled by the leaders and the management team profoundly shapes the culture of the organization. What leaders and managers emphasize, reward and routinely talk about sets the tone of the culture.

Some of the most visible expressions of the culture are the company's artifacts, things such as the architecture, the décor, the clothing people wear, the rituals, the symbols and the celebrations. Just look around the main lobby area to get clues.

Websense, a leader in security software solutions, is recognized as one of the fastest-growing small companies. Websense has a culture of winning—a culture of accomplishment. When you walk into the lobby, the décor strongly symbolizes this culture—the walls are lined with awards, citations and accolades that rein-force the culture of success.

Your corporate culture may become invisible to you over time. It sometimes takes an outsider such as a new customer, consultant or employee to identify your culture. Jennifer, a vice president, was new to her company. Bringing with her a fresh perspective and untainted point of view, she was able to identify the culture of the company quickly, seeing its strengths and its flaws. In a group conversation with other members of the executive team, Jennifer was the only one to suggest that the Excellence Thermostat in the company was below 50—compared to the above-70 setting her colleagues claimed. The other executives in the room wondered if Jennifer was being negative, or perhaps even funny. She went on to explain that their immersion in the culture had dulled their view, whereas she, as a newcomer, was able to see things the way they really are. Her comments were a reality check for the group and were instrumental in creating the climate for the many in-depth conversations about the company culture that later occurred among the group's members.

A culture of excellence is a culture of trust, integrity, respect, impeccable communication, maximum accountability, complete alignment, collaboration, cooperation, energy, vitality, joy, engagement and passion. The fundamental building blocks of a culture of excellence are the six Excellence principles. Use this book to implement the principles in a way that engages and inspires your team. You cannot force these principles, or change of any kind, on people. As you share these ideas with them, it will be up to you, and other Excellence champions in your organization, to create awareness of the possibility of how it *could be* to work in an environment in which everybody held themselves to the Excellence standards. When sharing these principles with groups, I see their eyes shining with excitement when they begin to realize how great their work life (and home life) could be if they, and the people around them, consistently applied the Excellence principles.

What is your organization's culture? If you were to describe it to an outsider, what words would you use? Think about what's really important, the behaviors that are rewarded and who fits in. A useful approach to clearly identifying your culture is to ask your employees what they say about your company when talking with their friends. In many cases, a company's culture has evolved over time, in an organic way, sometimes simply by default. Your job is to deliberately create your company's culture so that it reinforces your corporate goals, supports your strategic business imperatives and attracts great talent.

In his book *Re-imagine,* Tom Peters wrote, "Culture change is not 'corporate.' Culture change is not a 'program.' Culture change does not take 'years.' Culture change starts 'today.' It starts right now, and it is entirely in your hands!"

Step Two: Develop Excellent Managers

To be an employer-of-choice organization, you must develop Excellent Managers. Excellent Managers are role models of your culture of excellence who consistently reinforce and reward excellent behaviors. If managers gossip and dodge account-ability, and if they are unfocused, stressed out and joyless, their direct reports will follow suit. If, on the other hand, managers communicate impeccably, operate at the highest levels of accountability, are engaged and are effective, their attitudes will pervade the organization and set the standard for their employees.

Managers are the key to an employee's work experience. Studies from the Saratoga Institute ("The Emerging Workforce," 1997) confirm that 50 percent of employee satisfaction is determined by employees' relationship with the supervisor, and one of the top reasons employees leave is a breakdown in this relationship.

The adage *"Employees quit a boss, not a company"* is alive and well in the area of work-life balance. It is usually the employee's direct manager or supervisor that grants (or turns down) an employee's attempt to find flexibility with his or her job. (*Workforce Engagement*, 2007, WorldatWork Press.) In the 2004-2005 Performance Assessment Network national benchmark study, four in 10 employees could not agree that their manager recognizes the importance of their personal and family life.

Many managers have been promoted based on their technical expertise. In the past, this was acceptable. Today, technical expertise is no longer adequate. As an employer of choice, your managers need to understand and be dedicated to balancing their technical responsibilities and drive to achieve results with the required commitment to talent-relationship management.

Author Nancy S. Ahlrichs believes that talent-relationship management is the "new frontier." In the new workplace, managers will need to be held accountable for creating a culture in which people feel motivated, cared about and rewarded.

Most managers currently lack people-management skills, and most organiza-tions are thus at a severe disadvantage. Companies that dedicate resources to development of Excellent Managers will have competitive advantage. Guidelines to develop Excellent Managers include the following:

1. Set a new standard for management competency. Identify specific skills and competencies that managers will need to have in order to be competitive.

2. Identify learning and development programs that will effectively give managers the skills they need to become experts at attracting, optimizing and retaining talent.

3. Implement processes (e.g., regular results meetings in which participants report on outcomes) to ensure accountability for managers' application of those skills and competencies and for progress they're made in achieving company goals. Including the new competencies as part of the annual performance-review process will ensure managers stay on track.

4. Measure results using key indicators that your company considers important to the success of your business. Report these results to key stakeholders and link them to your business goals.

5. Reward managers for desired behaviors.

(For more on the Qualities of Excellent Managers, see Chapter 14.)

Step Three: Enlighten Leadership

When you establish a culture of excellence and commit to being an employer of choice, you are requiring your leaders to be enlightened. The personality and behaviors of your leaders set the tone for the rest of the organization. When we do business with a company, we can immediately tell by the way we are treated by the frontline employees whether the leaders of that company are enlightened or not.

Enlightened leaders are brilliant role models of the Excellence principles, supporters of Excellent Managers and rigorous enforcers of your employer-of-choice practices. In addition, they have mastered high-level leadership skills. Leaders are always being scrutinized and judged, even when they are not looking! Failure to live and breathe the Excellence principles can cause a loss of respect and credibility.

As one responder commented in an annual employee-opinion survey, "I had high hopes for our Excellence initiative. It was easy to buy into the principles because they were so in line with the company I originally had joined years ago. Sadly, it now seems a bit of a joke. I truly bought into the concepts and lessons until it became obvious that it was only meant for the regular employees, not management, even though they themselves participated in the program. Management and senior leaders in particular rarely demonstrate the lessons taught in the class, which makes it very difficult to want to aspire to the same goals. Having the company harp to its employees about the importance of Excellence simply rings hollow."

Enlightened leadership lies not in a powerful position or impressive job title but in the countless daily actions and behaviors that are an expression of the leader's character. Self-mastery is at the root of enlightened leadership—the authentic acknowledgment that self-awareness and continued development is key to leading a business.

Has your senior leadership team made it known (through deeds, not words) that truly exceptional leadership habits are expected of all managers, even those who, for a while at least, appear to be getting some pretty good business results? In other words, have they made it clear that there will be no hiding behind the numbers, and that folks who haven't really bought into the "leadership thing" have to either change or leave? (Bill Catlette, "Employer of Choice? Let's get real." *Workforce Management*.)

In a meeting with the general manager of a large space and defense company, it became apparent that I had encountered an enlightened leader. The purpose of the meeting had been to discuss implementation of the Excellence principles at the middle-management level. But the conversation soon turned into a discussion about the need for leadership development. He understood that the first step to becoming an employer of choice was for his leadership team to achieve mastery. When that had been accomplished, it would make sense to invest time and resources in the development of middle managers and line employees.

Lance Secretan, author and master teacher, has developed a set of principles that define enlightened leadership using the initialism, CASTLE: Courage, Authenticity, Service, Truthfulness, Love and Effectiveness. The CASTLE Principles are timeless truths that have always been part of what it takes to be a great leader. (More information about these principles can be found in Secretan's book, *One, The Art and Practice of Conscious Leadership*.)

The following points are a paraphrase of Secretan's definitions of the CASTLE qualities, and show how they fit within the Excellence paradigm.

- Courage: Enlightened leaders have the courage to go beyond limitations, fears and outmoded beliefs. They are willing to take the necessary action to initiate change.
- Authenticity: Enlightened leaders are fully present in all aspects of their lives. They are authentic, vulnerable and willing to be real.
- Service: Enlightened leaders know that their job is to be of service to others and to identify and meet the needs of their employees. They inspire others by their example.
- Truth: Enlightened leaders listen to others and are willing to accept the truth. They refuse to stay stuck in denial, even when the truth is painful. They are the very definition of integrity.
- Love: Enlightened leaders relate to others, regardless of their position in the company. They treat their employees with respect, kindness and love, and adhere to the maxim: "Do unto others as you would have them do unto you."
- Effectiveness: Enlightened leaders set high standards, and they are effective in achieving both their professional and personal goals.

Step Four: Align People Processes

It's important to align all your people processes with your culture of excellence and other employer-of-choice practices so that they are a strong expression of your employment brand. That is, all of your recruitment and selection, performance management, compensation and benefits processes must be built on a foundation of integrity, trust and respect. Only then can they help you attract top talent, optimize their performance and promote retention.

Leaders who believe in the Total Rewards philosophy will recognize these elements and understand the importance of aligning organizational processes so that excellence is the standard throughout the institutional or corporate culture. Let's examine the key elements of Total Rewards:

- Compensation: Traditionally thought to be the most important incentive for employee recruitment and retention, competitive pay (including short- and long-term incentive pay) remains a necessity for business success.

- Benefits: As businesses try to redefine the traditional benefits programs, such programs continue to be a key incentive for employees because they offer protection from financial risk and unforeseeable life events. In addition to providing standard health and retirement benefits, some companies are experimenting with nontraditional programs such as identity theft and pet insurance.

- Work-life: Programs that help employees balance their personal and professional lives have become the "secret sauce" in the recipe for business success (*workspan*, April 2006). Job sharing, telecommuting, gym memberships, educational opportunities and social events for families are among the programs that businesses use to help employees find a healthy balance in their lives.

- Performance and Recognition: When individual goals are aligned with organizational goals, performance is optimized. And optimal performance should be recognized. Recognition reinforces excellent performance and fosters positive communication. Compensation is one way to recognize performance, but you will learn about other effective forms of recognition in later chapters.

- Development and Career: Businesses and employees benefit when employees are allowed opportunities for growth. Advancement, changes in responsibilities and training enhance careers and contribute to employee engagement. Employees are stimulated and challenged; leaders have more time to devote to the company.

Mary-Ann Ellis, Alliance consultant, spearheaded the redesign of the performance-management process for a large public agency that was committed to becoming a world-class organization. The agency had realized that its performance-management process was founded on outdated principles and was cumbersome. It was dreaded by managers and employees alike and did little to meet the goal of performance management, which is to improve performance. Ellis applied some of the best practices shown in the "To" column in Figure 12-2 on page 137 at the agency in an effort to bring its performance-management system up to an employer-of-choice level.

To align your people processes, begin by asking the following questions:

1. Do they serve to attract top talent?
2. Do they optimize talent?
3. Do they inspire and influence top talent to stay?
4. Do they build trust and respect?
5. Do they reward desired behaviors (e.g. innovation, quality focus, teamwork, etc.)?
6. Do they reflect and reinforce the basic Excellence principles?

Step Five: Create Value

This is the final element of the Excellent Workplace Model. The two aspects to creating value are:

- Creating a workplace in which people have growth opportunities, a sense of meaning and a feeling of belonging. This type of workplace can be created through mentoring programs, career opportunities and community events that give people the chance to express and honor their values. As mentioned in the beginning of this book, there is a distinct trend toward a values-driven workplace in which employees are socially conscious and want to work for an organization that is supportive of that intent. At LexisNexis, for example, employees are given two paid days per year to participate in community-service activities such as Habitat for Humanity.

- Gaining recognition and building your reputation as an employer of choice. Accomplishing that takes some planning and effort, but the payoff is worth it! When you are recognized as a top employer, it is easier for you to attract top talent. By posting awards and recognitions on your Web site, at career fairs and in job advertisements, you will draw attention to your company as a great place to work.

Many organizations and publications offer Employer of the Year awards, Best Place to Work awards and Work Life Balance awards. Begin gaining recognition by applying for membership in local professional and trade associations. Even some newspapers sponsor these kinds of awards. When your company receives an award for workplace excellence, make sure you spread the word.

I was listening to a radio show on National Public Radio (NPR) recently, and when the underwriter of the show was announced, the company's name (North Highland, a consulting firm) was followed by a sentence touting its recognition as a "2006 Best Places to Work" by the *Tampa Bay Business Journal*. That brief mention will likely pique the interest of both job candidates and potential customers.

The following guidelines can help you to build your reputation as an employer of choice:

1. Develop and understand your message. What's the news?
   - Highlight awards, nominations, recognition and special designations.
   - Focus on personnel news such as new hires.
   - Describe unique programs, milestones and learning initiatives.
2. Identify your sources of information. Who will help you tell your story? Are they media-ready?

Figure 12-2:

People Processes – From and To

From	To
One-way, manager-driven process.	Joint discussion in which both parties prepare and influence the agenda, and in which employee self-review is a critical input step.
Postmortem, looking back and emphasis on discussion of past failures.	Looking forward and planning for improved performance.
Manager's role is judging and grading, which establishes an adult-to-child relationship.	Ratings are de-emphasized, with fair, equitable and easily understood criteria. The conversation is adult to adult.
Unclear goals and job expectations.	SMART (specific, measurable, accessible, realistic, timed) goals based on company goals that are aligned vertically and horizontally.
One manager's view.	Evaluation includes community feedback from employee's peers and internal customers.
An annual event.	Ongoing conversations with quarterly check-ins.
No link to employee development.	Development planning is an integral part of performance management.

- Prepare your CEO, human resources director, employees or others who can best help tell your story.

3. Identify targets for your message. What internal and external audiences will care, and why?
   - Internal: Employees are your best evangelists. Target your message to reach them so that they can then tell others why your company is such a great place to work.
   - External: Target the media, prospective employees and recruitment targets, current and prospective customers, professional associations and other influencers.

4. Plan and execute the pitch correctly. What to do and not to do when reaching out to the media:
   - Know your message and its true news value.
   - Know the media outlet and best person to pitch to.

5. Leverage media placements. Move up the media food chain:
   - Begin with trade media and then approach local media. When you have succeeded at a local level, pitch your story to regional media and, eventually, the national media.

6. Spread the good news. Tell the world about your efforts:
   - Post news on your Web site on your home page, your job openings page and your press page.
   - Prepare reprints for recruitment efforts.
   - E-mail the news to customers, influencers, etc.

(Bob Scheid, Principal, Forefront Communications)

Start Right Where You Are

Becoming an employer of choice may seem like a daunting task. Use the Excellent Workplace Model to guide your efforts. Begin by gathering support from others in your organization. Host a series of meetings to focus on what's possible for your company, where you would like to go and what it will take to get there. People don't resist change itself, but they do resist being changed and they resist changing. The only way to make progress is to contact, involve and enroll others in your vision.

Implementing Your Employer-of-Choice Strategy

John J. Cotter, Alliance consultant and acclaimed author of *The Twenty Percent Solution*, has created useful guidelines for implementing your employer-of-choice strategy.

The following poem by John J. Cotter says it perfectly:

I've always thought it rather strange
that those who plan and plead for change
do seldom contact or involve
the people upon whose resolve
success and failure rides and falls.

Without their help, the process stalls.
They fear to talk with everyone,
for this takes time and ain't much fun.

Still, if they don't, they'll mourn and wail,
'cause in the end, they'll likely fail.

My working theory is quite brief -
"Involve 'em, or you'll come to grief."

First, he suggests that you identify important stakeholders in your organization—key influencers whose support you will need. Identify whether they are supporters, opposers, allowers or preventers. Decide how best to mobilize them in support of your vision to become an employer of choice. Next, look for things that are already changing in your organization, positive and negative, that you can use to your advantage to achieve your goal of becoming an employer of choice. Before you institute additional changes, examine previous change experiences to learn how best to approach implementation of an employer-of-choice initiative. Be sure to deal with people's fears and concerns. Finally, build collaborative relationships with other work units, departments and employees.

John J. Cotter's guidelines for implementing your employer-of-choice strategy are:
- If possible, introduce new ideas on a small scale first, with the understanding

that they'll be expanded throughout the company later on. The intent is not to "see if they work" but to learn how to make them work effectively.

- Sites for prototypes should be chosen for their receptivity to learning the concepts, not their likely resistance to them.
- Treat mistakes as opportunities for learning, not as events to punish or ignore. Make sure the learning loop gets closed quickly while experiences are still fresh in people's minds.
- Deal with emerging issues promptly. Don't allow dissatisfaction and frustration to fester. Some frustration is helpful as a prelude to learning, but it can easily be overdone.
- Provide formal training as needed during the implementation phase instead of trying to get it over with all at once in the beginning. Skills and concepts can be acquired more effectively when there's some previous context in which to assess their usefulness.
- Design training around specific, identified needs instead of using existing, packaged programs. The training focus should be developmental rather than remedial, because people tend to embrace the former while resisting the latter.
- When replacing people who leave, retire or are promoted, as much as possible, hire people who possess the personal philosophy and capabilities called for by the change initiative.
- Provide constant high-visibility feedback on what's going right. Avoid publicizing only problems and failures. Create special events to celebrate specific achievements.
- Evaluate progress from the beginning of the implementation and don't be afraid to introduce corrections if change elements are not working as planned.
- Don't overstructure the details of implementation. Doing so limits opportunities for initiative and learning by those involved. It also incorrectly presupposes that every detail can be planned in advance.
- If the change moves too quickly, many employees will be left behind. They'll thus be unsure about the purpose and detail of what's likely to be implemented and unable to frame appropriate questions to express their concerns.
- Resistance by itself is neither good nor bad. It may be based on good reasons or not. Resistance, like pain, doesn't tell what's wrong; it only demonstrates that something *may* be wrong. It's always a signal that further inquiry is advisable.
- Try to reframe "I don't want to change" into "It won't work for me because..." Then deal with the "because."

chapter 13

Operationalizing Excellence

Pattie Vargas, Alliance consultant, first encountered the Excellence principles as a workshop participant. She was the manager of software development at her company, and she integrated them into her own department.

"Because we were an internal development team, we never got resources or a lot of attention. What we did was necessary but not sexy," Pattie said.

It was important for her to create a cohesive unit. The employees who worked under her had to get along and share a vision, or nothing would ever get done. In addition, they had to collaborate with other departments that had conflicting priorities and agendas. She saw how the Excellence principles could be a practical and tangible way for the engineers in her department to increase their effectiveness.

The first thing Pattie did to operationalize the principles was to charter a group of her employees with becoming cultural advocates for the Excellence principles. The TIPSI team—Training Into Practice Solutions and Ideas—established a goal: to lock in excellence. They developed a mission statement and came up with unique ways to bring the Excellence principles to the forefront of everyone's mind.

"At every staff meeting, we set aside 10 minutes for the TIPSI team to bring one of the principles to life," Patti said. "One time the team staged a mock TV game show. The commentator would read out a behavior, and the rest of us had to say whether it was accountable or unaccountable. Another time, they brought a piñata to demonstrate the principle *Lighten Up*. At the end of the meeting, 20 adults went out into the parking lot and began swinging at a Sponge Bob piñata full of silly stuff. Everyone had so much fun. It only took 15 minutes away from the workday, but after that everyone was energized and excited, full of camaraderie. There were people from other departments standing in the parking lot wishing they could be part of our team. It was a wonderful moment."

In addition to the creation of the TIPSI team, the IT team kept a flip chart posted in the hallway. Someone would write an Excellence principle in the middle of the page, and then others would add a thought about it whenever they felt like it. The page would be full by the end of the day with people's thoughts—sometimes silly, sometimes profound. But the effect was that the Excellence principles became embedded in their day-to-day conversations.

In their weekly meetings, the employees would traditionally discuss challenges they were facing. In discussing an obstacle he had encountered, one of the engineers clearly explained how he had used the Excellence principles.

He had an appointment with the architecture team, whose role had almost become synonymous with "roadblock." Team members were always going to ask for more, always going to say no, no matter what. That's what he had come to expect. The engineer went to the meeting with a negative attitude, but he remembered the Excellence principles and chose to "mine the gold." He decided he needed to figure out what the architecture team needed and what value it brought to the table. So instead of saying, "Here's my plan," he said, "Here's what I'm thinking of doing—do you think it will work?" The team members needed someone to validate them. When he did that, they became collaborative. He sailed through the process.

Pattie's department had been the only department in the company that implemented the Excellence principles, but the effect had been contagious. Employees from other departments had noticed the flip chart and began to record their own thoughts, too.

"It was a passive way of stating what we stood for," Pattie said. "We incorporated the principles into our department values, and they became part of our overall performance evaluations."

Though the company as a whole did not embrace the principles, Pattie's department was a small oasis of excellence. She was able to shield her department from the negativity and dysfunctionality of the rest of the company and create a happy, productive environment.

Pattie also noticed that she and others in her department began to apply the principles in their personal lives, as well.

"There's no division," she says. "It really is who you are. If you're excellent at work, then you're excellent everywhere."

To cultivate a culture of excellence for long-term organizational change, you must implement a comprehensive, customized plan to support and lock in the Excellence principles. This chapter includes specific strategies for integrating the Excellence principles into every aspect of your day-to-day operations.

Why Operationalize the Excellence Principles?

Any new concept, regardless of the quality of the program in which it's delivered or its initial effect on the participant, must be put into action or it will fail to yield lasting results. When you have introduced the principles into your organization, you will then want to employ strategies that will ensure that a firm foundation exists. Only in that way can ongoing, dynamic change occur.

As the principles become a part of their day-to-day behavior, your employees will begin to expand their circle of influence with their teammates, customers and business partners, which will lead to greater effectiveness of everyone. Even those who have not learned the concepts will be affected by the quality of the communication of those employees who are committed to a new way of doing business.

The first step in operationalizing is to form one or more Excellence Champion Groups. Identify key employees who are committed to the possibility of excellence. They can be self-nominated or nominated by others. The Excellence Champion Group can strategize ways to operationalize excellence. Allow it to institute new practices, rituals and routines. Its very existence will be a constant reminder of excellence. While we provide many examples of strategies in this chapter and throughout the book, offer employees the chance to unleash their creativity in creating new ones.

The following is a step-by-step process to operationalize the Excellence principles:

1. *Identify "champions" to make up the Excellence Champion Group:*
   - The team should include key decision makers to assist in implementation and to ensure the program has team support. The team will quickly become discouraged if there is no relevant feedback or if it is unable to move forward on a particular action due to slow decision-making or approvals.
   - Team members should be willing participants. The purpose of the program is not to convince the team participants of the value of excellence—the members should be advocates, willing to champion the cause.

2. *Hold Strategy Sessions*
   - The first strategy session is to establish the team, determine its purpose (create a team name and mission statement) and agree on what it wishes to accomplish. It is important that a *team* deliverable be established so there's a goal to be accountable for. The use of time lines and action items will reinforce the importance of the sessions.
   - The second strategy session is to keep the team on track and to offer guidelines and assistance in pulling it back in line if it has become discouraged or sidetracked. New ideas for using *Principle #6 - Lighten Up* should be

discussed, and plans should be made. Fun is a great motivator and will keep the team motivated and enthusiastic. The time line should be reviewed for adherence. A final presentation should be discussed and planning should be started—knowing that *something* will be presented to *someone* also reinforces the importance of the team and its work. Who it is presented to will vary from organization to organization.

- The third strategy session reviews progress and discusses the upcoming presentation. The purpose is to establish that this new behavior has become part of the organization and is sponsored by the people in the organization.

3. *Follow up*
   - Schedule a breakfast or lunch session with the team and invited stakeholders who participated in the team's presentation.
   - At this session, a designated leader should review the six Principles of Excellence and offer specifics about how the team expanded the understanding of each principle among employees.
   - Facilitate discussions on challenges and new opportunities for expanding the new code of conduct. Encourage the participation of the managers or stakeholders in the discussions.

Excellence is a state of mind. The changes you will see as you begin to operationalize the Excellence principles will be subtle but also distinctive and powerful. Notice how members of the team manage themselves and their communications differently. Next, pay attention to how excellence infiltrates all levels of the organization.

Suggestions for Team Implementation

- Have brown-bag lunch meetings with other departments or teams within the organization to spread the word.
- Use contests to "catch" someone being excellent. Award some type of prize or recognition.
- Foster competition between departments—softball games, water gun fights, etc.—that encourage camaraderie and goodwill.
- Offer lunchtime showings of videos with themes about excellence—these could be inspirational or fun.
- Post the Excellence principles in visible locations—this could be in whatever format fits the organizational culture, from professionally mounted to methods that demonstrate creativity and personality.
- Develop an Excellence Web site where one principle can be showcased each month, tips can be posted and employees can share ideas and challenges.

- Make the principles a part of a departmental mission statement—they may not be able to cause change at the level of the corporate mission statement, but they could have influence more locally.

Keeping Excellence in the Forefront

In addition to appointing a team—or if you are a member of the team—you will want to keep the principles in the forefront of everyone's consciousness.

Think of it as a three-layer approach:

- *Layer one: Passive reminders:*
  - Screen savers, weekly or monthly e-mail, and posters on Excellence
- *Layer two: Activities*
  - Competitions, conversations and other activities focused on the principles
- *Layer three: Reward and recognition*
  - Acknowledgment of individuals who demonstrate excellence.

To recognize excellent behavior, you might create Excellence Recognition Cards. You can hold a drawing and offer a prize to one of the recipients. The peer group needs to be aware of these activities and on the lookout for these behaviors. Remember, you get the behavior you reward. So when employees are recognized by their peers when they excel, they will be encouraged to repeat the behavior.

Debbie, a CIO, inherited an IT department with a negative attitude. The typical response to requests for IT help from other departments was simply, "No!" The department had become so used to this behavior that it had become deeply ingrained. Even when a simple request was made, people immediately dismissed it. Debbie was committed to changing her team's behavior but at a loss as to how to accomplish her goal. I suggested she reinforce a "yes" attitude by asking employees from other departments to recognize IT staff every time it offered great customer service and responded positively to a request. Debbie developed a series of "YES!" recognition cards that were awarded to the IT staff every time it said "yes" to an IT request. The initiative was a big success and resulted in positive behavior change, and employees had fun, too.

The Challenge

The biggest challenge to operationalizing the principles is getting commitment. Ideally, a key stakeholder will be the driving force behind it. Look for ways to get key stakeholders to champion the efforts. Show them the benefits of an organization geared to excellence in terms of employee recruitment and retention as well as performance and profitability.

In addition, use the principles to drive your own personal behavior. The more enlightened you become, the more enlightened people around you tend to become. People who show up around you will know that they are held up to higher standards and will behave accordingly.

chapter 14

Qualities of Excellent Managers

Management today is very different from what it used to be. Many of today's managers learned how to manage from their own managers, who weren't necessarily expert people managers or even expected to be. While the measure of a good manager used to be the bottom line, managers today are measured by both their results and their ability to attract, optimize and retain talent. Managers in the past might have asked, "How will I meet my numbers?" or "What do I need to get the project done?" Now they are asking, "How I can attract the best talent, inspire them to contribute at the highest levels and keep them?"

The Excellent Manager has a new mind-set. He or she approaches management from a different point of view than did managers in the past. Today's manager understands that if one intends to be effective, one must balance the drive for results with expert people-management skills. Figure 14-1 on page 148 compares management in the past to management today and specifies the kind of thinking required to effectively manage in the new workplace.

Excellent Managers Have a Strong Brand

Excellent Managers have a strong leadership brand—an identity or reputation for being both great technicians and expert people managers. Dave Ulrich, professor of business administration at the University of Michigan, and Norm Smallwood wrote that "leadership brand represents the identity and reputation of leaders throughout a company." They also noted that strong and effective leaders at all levels contribute to an organization's overall business results (Link&Learn, March 2006).

Your leadership brand is a declaration of who you are and what you are committed to individually (and collectively) as a leader in your organization. Your leadership brand should express the value you want to offer, the things you would like to accomplish and the kind of person (and people) you want to be known as. It is a proclamation of what matters most to you. This brand helps you to attract high performers both internal and external to the organization.

Figure 14-1:

Managers—Then and Now

Then	Now
Think of their staff as **employees**	Think of their staff as **talent**
Believe people are **important**	Know people are **everything**
Think of training as a **department**	See training as a **necessity**
Are **drivers**	Are **facilitators, mentors and talent miners**
Focus on bottom-line **results**	Focus on **results and people**
Are good **technicians**	Are good technicians and brilliant talent **managers**
Are required to have **some people skills**	Must be **expert people managers**
Rely on human resources for recruitment, selection and on-boarding	**Partner with HR** to recruit, select and on-board
Believe **one-size management** fits all	Are **versatile** and committed to meeting the unique needs and demands of a multiethnic, four-generation workforce
Feel turnover is **expected**	Actively **manage retention**
Are accountable for **results**	Are accountable for **results and talent management**
Tolerate people-management responsibilities	Are **dedicated** people managers
Aware of employee **satisfaction** levels	Rigorously manage **engagement**
Hope top producers will stay	**Actively** manage retention through "stay interviews"
Conduct infrequent, **tactical** one-on-one meetings with direct reports	Conduct frequent, **strategic** one-on-one meetings to discuss direct reports' goals, aspirations and future plans

Your leadership brand must be congruent with your company's brand and be consistent among all managers in your company. It should be reflected in your daily actions and behaviors, and should also be reinforced by your decisions. You must live and breathe your brand or risk loss of credibility. Every broken promise or misaligned action will threaten the strength of your leadership brand.

What is your leadership brand? Does it enable you to attract and retain top talent? Does it strengthen or weaken your company brand?

Excellent Managers are Talent Experts

As an Excellent Manager, you are dedicated to talent management, and you balance your technical responsibilities with your commitment to managing your people. Take the following quiz to find out if you are an Excellent Manager.

Do you:

- Have a talent strategy—an accurate assessment of who is on your team, who are your top performers and who you will need to meet your goals?
- Have a consistent reputation for being a great manager?
- Have an agreement and mechanism in your company to share talent with other departments?
- Actively scout for talent externally?
- On-board new talent in a way that quickly integrates them and establishes a sense of belonging?
- Have a published set of guiding principles for your team that you hold them accountable to?
- Train or retrain your employees for highest performance?
- Build strong, connected relationships with each direct report and between direct reports?
- Reward achievement consistently and appropriately?
- Architect a distinctive team culture free of toxic behaviors, passion busters and productivity blocks?
- Inspire passion and engagement in each member of your team?
- Influence loyalty, pride and a sense of meaning?
- Inquire regularly what will keep your people in the organization by means of stay interviews, and then take continuous action to retain talent?

If you answered "yes" to all the questions above, you are an Excellent Manager.

Extracting the Gold

On a recent trip to visit members of my family in South Africa, my 11-year-old son and I had the opportunity to go down into a working gold mine. That was the highlight of our vacation as well as an important learning experience for me. As we descended 600 feet down into the mine in a steel cage packed tightly with tourists like us, I was reminded of the similarity between a gold miner and an Excellent Manager.

Gold miners are relentless, fearless and disciplined in their craft—and they work tirelessly to extract the gold from the rock. Similarly, Excellent Managers demonstrate an unbridled passion and commitment to extracting the very best from their employees. In doing so, they set themselves apart. If you have been down in a mine, you will know that the physical conditions are extremely tough. It is hot, humid, damp, dark and very noisy. In the case of the mine we visited, miners typically traveled up to two hours each day in the elevator to reach their shaft. In some cases they were paid as little as $2 per day. In some organizations, it would seem that the job of people management is no less daunting. Is it common in your company for managers to sometimes avoid their talent-mining function because they perceive it to be too challenging, uncomfortable or perhaps unnecessary?

Gold miners rejoice in their success. Though they must mine up to three tons of ore to extract a single ounce of gold, at the end of each day they celebrate their efforts by singing and dancing. What would it be like if, at the end of each workday, you and your fellow managers celebrated your people management efforts by rejoicing in the knowledge that your talent-mining activities would have significant payoff? As the CEO of a software company said to his management team, "Integrating these Excellence principles and becoming expert talent managers will enable us to positively affect the triple bottom line and help us become the vendor of choice, the investment of choice and the employer of choice." Wise words!

Excellent Managers are talent magnets, talent miners and talent keepers

Excellent Managers are expert in three critical competencies:

- Attracting talent
- Optimizing talent
- Retaining talent.

In the past, managers were expected to hire the right person for the right job at the right time. Today's managers need to devise strategies to find great talent and then attract that talent to work for them. When you become a talent magnet, internal talent and prospective talent seek you out and choose to work for you. Not satisfied with just having made a good hire, you act tirelessly to integrate the new employee and launch him or her as quickly and effectively as you can to achieve full optimization.

Performance management has been an important focus for managers, who are required to offer regular coaching and feedback as well as a meaningful annual performance review. These fundamental management competencies will always be important. But in the changing workplace, the demand on managers will be to optimize talent, not just manage it. In other words, managers will need to be "talent miners." A talent miner, just like a gold miner, has a deep commitment to helping his or her employees achieve breakthrough performance.

Management training in the 1980s and 1990s emphasized the need to motivate employees. While traditional motivation theories are still valid, today's Excellent Manager understands that job No. 1 is to engage the hearts and minds of all employees so that they will perform at their highest levels in pursuit of their performance goals. Excellent Managers are talent keepers. They know that maintaining employee satisfaction, while interesting and useful, is not nearly as important as actively managing engagement.

It's All About Engagement

What is the difference between employee satisfaction and engagement? A satisfied employee likes his job and work environment. An engaged employee will do what it takes to achieve the business result. Sometimes we fall into the trap of believing that a satisfied employee is a highly productive employee, and that a high level of satisfaction will automatically lead to retention. That's not the case at all. You might have noticed there are some employees in your company who are quite happy but are certainly not high performers. One is not engaged because one stays; one stays because one is engaged.

With more than 1,800 employees representing public, private and not-for-profit organizations, the 2006-2007 *National Benchmark Study on Workforce Engagement* collected results that paint a darker picture for today's employers than the study conducted two years ago. In 2006-2007, only 40 percent of all employees are fully engaged with their organization, a significant decrease in engagement from 2004-2005's level of 46 percent.

With nearly as many employees pushing against their company as are pulling for them, and one in four feeling reluctant to leave and reluctant to work hard, the the same national benchmark study not only shows employee engagement and retention more at risk, it shows customer satisfaction, repeat purchase and the company's financial health at risk, as well. (Hundley, et al, 2007)

The following studies point to a definitive link between engagement and retention and also show that engagement leads to improved performance:

- A Development Dimensions International (DDI) study of a *Fortune* 100 manufacturing company showed that low-engagement teams averaged 14.5-percent turnover and 8-percent absenteeism, while high-engagement teams had 4.1-percent turnover and 4.8-percent absenteeism. Quality errors were 5,658 for the low-engagement group, compared to 52 for the high-engagement group
- A Hewitt and Associates study showed that in companies where 60 percent to 70 percent of employees were engaged, average total shareholder return (TSR) was 24.2 percent. Companies with 50-percent to 60-percent employee engage-

ment showed 9.1 percent TSR. Companies with engagement below 25 percent suffered negative TSR.

- The Corporate Executive Board surveyed 50,000 employees in 59 organizations worldwide. The data showed that employees with lower engagement are four times more likely to leave their jobs than those who are highly engaged. This same study showed that moving from low to high engagement can result in a 21-percent increase in performance.

Excellent Managers are Accountable for Talent Management

In a conversation with a group of managers at a successful consumer products company, I asked how they measure their effectiveness. One manager responded by saying that a key indicator of her success is that she can go away for a few days and return and find that everything is still okay. Another manager suggested that a key measure of his success is that his direct reports are able to make decisions on their own. Both are good answers but fail to objectively measure management effectiveness. The true measure of an Excellent Manager is his or her results.

An Excellent Manager is measured by the following criteria:

- Has a strong reputation that attracts top candidates to seek positions in the company
- Influences top candidates to accept a position in the company
- Inspires current employees to refer qualified job candidates
- Minimizes the number of bad hires who terminate or quit within the first 12 months of employment
- Maintains a high level of employee engagement
- Ensures employees participate in relevant, actionable training each year
- Architects internal promotions for top talent
- Actively mentors key talent
- Conducts a meaningful annual performance review for employees to inspire improved performance and deepen engagement
- Achieves a high level of performance of new hires within six to 12 months after hire
- Retains top talent
- Is not one of the top three reasons employees give for leaving in their exit interviews.

Excellent Managers Have Achieved Self-Mastery

Excellent Managers can be counted on to role model the Excellence principles in everything they do. They are held accountable for demonstrating these behaviors consistently. One of the ways that managers can consistently develop and maintain excellence is to seek 360-degree feedback on a regular basis to illuminate blind spots. Excellent Managers also participate in learning, reading and coaching to continuously improve their management and leadership skills. An Excellent Manager never rests on his or her past accomplishments. He or she knows that yesterday's definition of excellence is no longer valid.

Part 4

Winners of the Game:
Case Studies of Excellent Companies

chapter 15

Excellence at Quidel

In Part Four we'll look at some companies that have integrated excellence into their day-to-day operations. In this chapter and Chapter 16, we'll look at two very different types of organizations, both of which have been recognized for their excellence. Chapters 17, 18 and 19 each look at a company that has participated in the Excellence programs and examine how the company has incorporated the Excellence principles into its culture.

These stories of successful companies in which workers are passionate and committed to excellence have much in common. Employees are valued, and they know it. Negativity isn't tolerated. Leadership knows how to mine the gold. People are accountable, focused and balanced. They are excited about work and they know how to lighten up.

The first company we'll study went through a crisis in the first years of this decade. Under new leadership, Quidel examined its market share, its potential and its goals. The company soon developed a vibrant culture of excellence.

Quidel's Mission and Vision

Quidel Corp. develops and globally markets point-of-care, rapid diagnostic tests for infectious diseases and reproductive health. The company focuses primarily on physician office labs and acute-care markets. Quidel also develops diagnostic and research assays and reagents, through its Specialty Products Group, that have application in oncology, bone health and inflammatory diseases.

As far as the work environment is concerned, the company is "dedicated to providing employees with a great place to work and an environment that values team play and ethical behavior." There is a long history of, and demonstrated commitment to, quality at Quidel Corp. This commitment is reflected in the company's Quality Policy, which covers the quality of products and services as well as interactions with all customers, including employees.

"This commitment to quality is attained by listening to our internal and external customers, translating their needs into innovative solutions and taking a leadership role in all we do."

These statements are clearly aligned with the Excellence principles and provide a clear indication of why the company was the 2005 winner of the San Diego Society for Human Resources Workplace Excellence Award.

According to its vision statement, Quidel's goal is "to become the absolute, undisputed leader in delivering rapid diagnostic healthcare solutions at the point of care. Our ultimate and all-consuming mission is to enhance the health and well-being of people around the globe." Quite a tall order, is it not?

To maintain the highest level of quality, Quidel is committed to excellence in communication. Remember the first principle, *Use Your Word Wisely?* The corollary to that principle, of course, is to listen wisely. Quidel actively seeks out the opinions and ideas of its internal and external customers, and translates those needs into innovative solutions. The company leadership emphasizes the importance of teamwork and maintains a strong focus on continuous improvement. In other words, it is not content to settle for "good enough."

Quidel's Core Values

In their book *Built to Last: Successful Habits of Visionary Companies,* Jim Collins and Jerry I. Porras reported that one of the key variables found in successful companies is a set of strong core values. Quidel's core values are especially important in establishing a corporate culture. Notice the wording of the following values statements: "Our success is fueled by *our passion, knowledge and creativity.* We value team play, and we insist upon honesty and ethical behavior. We respect each other and the customers we serve [emphasis added]."

Of course, anyone can write down a list of high-minded ideals. The real key is to put those ideals into practice.

While compiling material for this book, I spoke to leaders at Quidel to get a sense of how their ideas worked in practice. The company had been under the leadership of Caren L. Mason, president and CEO since 2004.

According to Dina Purvis, manager, human resources, who had been with the company for 15 years at the time we spoke, Quidel had a distinct culture even before the recent change in leadership.

"Caren built on the foundation that was here, a foundation of people who are dedicated to the quality of the products and committed to the quality of customer service. Companies go through cycles in terms of culture development, and leadership has a lot to do with building a culture. With Caren we're not only hearing the right things, but we're also seeing them put into practice."

Purvis noted that Quidel has a number of long-term employees who know that they'll be held to a high level of performance. She has observed that people often want to work with the company because of the employees. New hires have told her that during the interview process, they could tell that the employees were passionate and excited about what they were doing and committed to being the best in the industry.

One of the important core values is valuing every employee's opinion. Mason and other members of leadership maintain an open-door policy. As was suggested in the chapter on operationalizing excellence, groups of employees at all levels are invited to meet with the CEO regularly. In those meetings anything and everything can be discussed.

"As a result of these meetings, we have upgraded our break rooms and now offer healthy-choice selections for those who wish to purchase lunch and snack foods at work," Mason said. On a tour of the Quidel facility, I noticed the break rooms have an unusual addition—a bookcase filled with books employees bring to share with each other. Since one of their core values is knowledge, it would follow that reading is promoted and encouraged.

When you create a culture of excellence, it must permeate every aspect of the organization, including the physical appearance. So the leaders at Quidel decided to refurbish the entire building, and they wisely made sure that employees were involved in the effort.

"We had the building painted and relandscaped," Mason said. "We had people get involved in the color selection. We redid the lobby and the carpeting and instituted a visitor protocol. We redid all our internal communications. We've become a vibrant, colorful, innovative, humanistic company."

Building on a Foundation of Excellence

When Mason came on board, she found that a foundation for excellence already existed as a result of the company's standing in the industry. The company had the awards and the market share to prove itself. However, senior leaders had different ideas about how to take the company to the next level.

"We had the underpinning, but didn't have cohesiveness. Everybody wasn't pulling in the same direction," she said.

Mason realized that having seven members of senior leadership was not enough. So the decision-making level of leadership was expanded so that it encompassed the director level and higher. This group now has functional ownership for creating the company's capabilities and delivering results.

Mason and the group of approximately 22 people went off site for a retreat in which they looked at their external data in order to understand where their growth opportunities were. The new leadership group realized that its performance was much higher than its competitors' but that it was important to provide the evidence.

"It's all about proof," Mason said. "We've branded quality. Now, we don't just talk about our performance. We provide the clinical and economic validation. This documentation becomes not just an internal proof. It goes to our customers, to the community in which we received the Workplace Excellence Award and into our recruitment materials."

When the leadership team decided upon the "underpinning theme" of Quidel Value Build™, it was able to build a mission and vision for the direction of the company.

"It took us five days to hammer it out," Mason said. "But we wanted to make sure it was absolutely right. We built some fun into it. We developed camaraderie and discussed what behaviors to reward and which would not be tolerated."

This was an important statement for the leadership to make. So often a company's leaders believe that their mission is to serve shareholders. They lose sight of what their real mission is. By focusing on expanding wellness globally, the leaders at Quidel had built in an intrinsic reward for the employees, because the employees know they are doing something important.

"We talk about that all the time—what our products really do, why they're so important," Mason said.

To solidify their position as the best in their field, the leaders built five "strategic imperatives." Four of those strategic imperatives revolved around operations, but importantly, the fifth strategic imperative was about culture: "Create and sustain a quality culture where we achieve all strategic imperatives, exemplify our values and celebrate our successes."

Key Alignments

The human resources department led by Phyllis Huckabee, VP Human Resources, built a Quidel incentive plan so that everyone in the organization was aligned, from the production floor to the top executives. The result is a culture of excellence.

"We've developed a terrific culture, in part because employees get excited as they see how their daily efforts are contributing to the overall success of the organization," Huckabee said. "Their compensation is directly linked to this success."

Employees at Quidel have evidence that if they live up to the standards of the company established in the strategic imperatives, they will not only be paid well but they will have fun, they will be introduced to new techniques and they will be encouraged to be creative.

"The first year was one of building trust and establishing positive relationships with the workforce," Mason said. Leadership communicates with employees at regular meetings on the strategic imperatives. Through both formal and informal discussions, all employees are able to track progress toward annual goals and adjust individual and functional work, as necessary.

"Whatever we adopt is bought into at the top level, and so we have a tight alignment. Everybody is marching in sync," she said.

In maintaining vigilance over companywide alignment, Quidel conducts a midyear review with all of its employees, including leadership. The review process matches the behaviors that leadership wants to encourage with the goals of the employee. The midyear review validates whether or not the employee has made the strategic imperative operating objectives that he or she agreed to.

"We take great pains that no one is ever surprised with their performance at any point," Mason said.

Even the top leadership is held accountable. Mason's performance review is with the board.

"Nobody skates," she said. "It's all fully aligned."

A Culture of Creativity

Mason remarked that underneath the structure there must be a sense of entrepreneurism if excellence is to truly be achieved. Employees must be allowed creativity in the way they meet their goals. Delivering results in a way that is consistent with Quidel's values is very important.

So during the review process, the supervisors not only describe whether or not employees met their goals but *how* they were able to meet them.

"We give you the opportunity to bring something new to the table. The way you perform to those goals is truly yours. We're trying to maintain a balance so that the processes in place do not stifle creativity," Mason said.

The culture of Quidel is one of vibrancy, fun and innovation. The level of energy is high because leadership is open to new ideas. Teamwork is effective because negative undercurrents (downward-spiral conversations) are not tolerated. The three C's of complaint, criticism and condemnation are not allowed.

"We want to know that you're a stellar individual when you work for Quidel," Mason said. "We expect absolute integrity and strong ethics."

As you saw in the chapter on the first Excellence principle, *Use Your Word Wisely,* language plays an important role in fostering creativity, and Quidel's corporate word choice reflects the attitude that permeates the workplace. For example, it uses the term "teamplay" rather than "teamwork," and "quality" is used in reference to the culture because "quality" should be top-of-mind as employees do their jobs.

"This is the message we want to deliver and that we want to live," Mason said.

Creating Excellence from Day One

You may think that Quidel has incredible luck in finding these stellar individuals, but in fact it has learned how to indoctrinate new hires into this culture of excellence, and new employees rise to meet the standards that are expected of them. While the human resources team at Quidel does a great job of selecting employees who have passion and drive, the underpinning of excellence tends to be contagious.

This indoctrination into a culture of excellence helps to attract top talent, retain top talent and bring out the best of each individual.

"On-boarding actually begins before anyone comes on board," said Sandy Agan, HR advisor at Quidel. "When we identify a candidate or résumé, we give that person a lot of attention. At the very first meeting, they know whom they are meeting and what their titles are. Everybody takes it seriously."

When the new person is hired, HR provides an assimilation memo so that the new employee already has an e-mail address, and someone is appointed to show the person around and introduce him or her to others. The orientation process reinforces the employee's decision to come to Quidel.

"There are a lot of things that can help with the on-boarding process. When they first come in, they're excited. You can either buoy it or kill it," Agan said.

During the first month of employment, employees attend an orientation meeting with the CEO, who inculcates them into the value system of Quidel. According to Agan and Huckabee, during orientations, new hires often remark that they accepted their positions because they had a chance to see cross-collaboration between leadership and staff during their interview process.

Top talent is starting to seek out Quidel because the recruiters exude the kind of passionate energy that draws talented individuals to the company.

"People want to come work for us. We've recruited people away from much larger, better-known corporations," Agan said.

Quidel's HR team has become adept at *Mining the Gold.* Sometimes in the interview process, Purvis noted, a candidate will have a certain skill set that may not be in the job description.

"We will build a job around the skill set when appropriate," Huckabee said. "That's exciting for people to see. We are creating a job for a real need the company has."

When an employee is hired, HR follows up with managers and the employees. The employees are asked about their on-boarding experience, and the managers are asked if the new hire is a good fit. This feedback provides the HR group with information about the job it is doing so it can continue to fine-tune the recruitment process.

Measuring the Results

It's easy for a company to call itself an employer-of-choice. But to really know whether or not you are an employer of choice, you must have measurable quantifiers. One way that Quidel measures its success is through employee surveys that ask about a variety of beliefs, attitudes and opinions.

"While 100-percent satisfaction is never the goal—we don't want complacency—we have a strong affinity for always looking at how we can improve and what we can do better," explained Huckabee.

This extends beyond survey results. The company's leaders also look at how well they are doing competitively. The compensation planning is extensive.

Training, development and coaching are ongoing.

"I believe in developing talent. We mentor our employees. We will hire a coach for someone who needs it. We pride ourselves on helping someone get to the next level," Mason said—another example of how *Mining the Gold* can be built into the system.

"Culture is expressed in everything you do. The culture is itself a magnet. The culture is about the people, and especially the leaders, being magnets," Mason said.

Quidel, obviously, has many things in its favor. But the strategies that leadership at Quidel has put into place and its commitment to excellence can be demonstrated within any organization. We'll look at three other companies and examine their strategies, as well.

chapter 16

A Hole in One: Troon Golf

The Excellence principles can be found in one form or another wherever an organization is striving for excellence. These organizations will be the leaders in their fields, regardless of the size of the organization. Whether it is a multinational corporation or a small family-owned business, a high set of standards supported by values and principles will set it apart from the competition.

One company that embraces excellence is Troon Golf, a company with approximately 8,000 employees. Headquartered in Scottsdale, Ariz., Troon Golf is the world's largest golf management company, overseeing operations at more than 185 courses located in 29 states and 18 countries. One of the company's core beliefs is: "The creativity and energy of our people stimulate a culture of enthusiasm, excellence and innovation."

Facility of the Year

Each year Troon recognizes "The Troon Golf Facility of the Year." In 2004, the facility that was recognized was Whirlwind Golf Club, which received the following accolades: "Whirlwind has continued to produce one of the most consistent, quality operations within Troon Golf. The Whirlwind team excelled in all aspects of golf and club operations to be named Facility of the Year."

The facility was also selected as one of the Top 100 Best Golf Shops for 2006 by *Golf World Business*. This award is given to "an elite group that exemplifies retail excellence in a remarkably competitive field," said Mark Murphy, editor of the magazine.

Peg Chapin, director of Golf at Whirlwind Golf Club, said that several qualities contribute to the overall excellence of the organization.

"We believe our associates are our source of strength," she said. "The person on the front line is the most important person in the company. They take care of the guests, and I take care of them."

The employees range in age from 19 to 60, and the older staff members often serve as mentors to the younger ones. Chapin said that because the standards among the employees are high, they bring new hires up to their level. The result is low turnover.

Chapin believes in treating her staff with respect and dignity. While her job title is different from theirs, she'll still get out with her staff and load golf carts during busy periods. She remarked that she never orders an employee to do something, but always asks. Expressing gratitude is one way she said that she uses her words wisely.

"I learned a long time ago that employees are going to act like their leaders," Chapin said. "I have to set an example. Nothing I'm doing is more important than their needs."

Recognizing Individual Excellence

The golf facility at Whirlwind Golf Club has an "on-the-spot" award that recognizes excellence. Any employee can recognize any other employee for going above and beyond the call of duty and for delivering excellent service.

"Of course, we also have Employee of the Month and Employee of the Year awards, but what's so great about the on-the-spot award is that it's given by anyone. As a manager, I can't be everywhere and see everything. Managers don't always have time to tell everyone 'you did a great job.' But this way, they still get recognized," Chapin explained. "We're really a team here."

Chapin and other managers at her resort are strong believers in *Mine the Gold*. For example, Chapin cited the case of a young man who wanted to be a golf pro but had no work experience.

"He had no idea how to clock in on time," Chapin said, laughing. "I began to hold him accountable for his behavior, and we saw a dramatic change. No one had ever told him how to go to work. He became responsible and became an assistant golf pro. He just sent me a thank you note.

"We coach and counsel first. We don't like letting people go."

Work-Life Balance

Chapin said that one of Troon's greatest strengths is the company's attitude about work-life balance. Being a golf resort makes it easy for the staff to have fun playing golf after hours. But management also provides tickets for other sporting events and numerous occasions for employees to bond socially.

Quarterly meetings don't have to be drudgery. At the quarterly meetings of the resort staff, the chef provides food (in addition to the requisite pizzas), and in addition to going over the financial figures for the quarter, employees break into groups, play games and give out prizes.

"It's a fun get-together," Chapin said.

While excellence at work is key, the company recognizes that sometimes life interferes with an employee's ability to work at his or her best.

"Leadership recognizes that life is about more than work. When someone has a personal issue—a death in the family or a sick child—then it's important for him or her to take care of it. We cover for each other when we need to," Chapin said.

Chapin experienced this compassionate perspective herself when she was diagnosed with cancer.

"My second day in the hospital, I received flowers from the vice president of the company. The company leaders did everything possible to make sure I could continue to work and still take care of my health. To this day, they make sure I am able to do my best and do what I need to do for me. I know that they care about me."

chapter 17

A Modern Model of Excellence: Modern Postcard

"As a CFO, my goal is to create value in the organiza-tion. The Excellence Program has helped to build an environment where people can be most effective, become as good as they are, and even better than they should be, thereby adding value. The program has served to decrease the human friction and establish an environment of creativity, innovation, trust and respect—all essential elements of a successful company. Modern Postcard's continued growth and increased profitability is proof we have achieved 'excellence.' Some might ask how we can afford to offer a program like this to our entire employee population. I ask, "How can we afford not to?"

—Bill Lofft, Former CFO

Background

When you are looking for Modern Postcard's headquarters, you might easily drive right by it. The unobtrusive gray sign "The Iris Group and Modern Postcard" is classic and unpretentious. Proceed up the driveway and be welcomed by a bright, airy and architecturally brilliant structure with precise attention to detail, style and aesthetics. Walk into the lobby and you immediately notice the openness—

every wall and door is glass, promoting the free flow of ideas and creativity and reinforcing a culture of collaboration, cooperation and openness. Young Generation X'ers and Y'ers are buzzing around doing their work and, by the way, having a lot of fun, too!

CEO Steve Hoffman prefers the unobtrusive street sign and simplicity of Modern Postcard's building. He focuses on delivering a high-quality product at a very competitive price. He also insists all employees enter the building every day through the back door and walk through the production facility, in which state-of-the-art presses hum around the clock. That's an interesting idea, you might think, especially since entering through the main lobby might be more pleasing. He does this, Hoffman says, because he wants employees to be reminded every day that the heart of the business is in the production facility, and to acknowledge the pressmen who produce an impeccable end product—high-quality, custom postcards.

Modern Postcard has been the industry leader for over a decade, serving more than 150,000 companies across 40 industries. They have printed more than 1 billion postcards for a variety of customers—from artists and marketing managers to gallery managers to medical products companies. When a company like Modern Postcard is already doing well, meeting its goals and thriving, it is often difficult to persuade key stakeholders to sit in a training room for the purposes of continued improvement. But for a vice president of human resources like Sarai Rodgers, ongoing development is key to the company's success. With trepidation, and sometimes-bated breath, she insisted that Modern Postcard's executive and management team, including the CEO, CFO and VP, had to participate in the Excellence program. Her passion and commitment to continually growing was rewarded by the subsequent overwhelming agreement of key stakeholders to initiate an enterprisewide Excellence initiative.

Over a two-year period, 150 employees from all departments, including sales, marketing, finance and even mailing services participated in a series of learning experiences, real-world case studies and practical application activities and practical application. They immersed themselves in the conversation about what they were committed to, how they could be even better than they are and how they wanted to be known in their industry.

Integration of Excellence Principles

Rodgers and her HR team, in conjunction with Customer Service Manager Lorena Abood, were absolutely committed to making sure the Excellence principles didn't just become a passing fad and "flavor of the month." They wanted the learning and discovery to stay with people and become fully integrated into the day-to-day-work environment. They focused on rewarding and recognizing excellent behaviors by using the Excellence principles in a variety of creative ways, including as the basis for their national Customer Service Week celebrations. Each day they offered creative reminders, activities and rewards for employees who demonstrated the principle of the day.

Because the company is in the business of creating postcards, Rodgers developed attractive, inspirational cards for each principle and specific tips. For instance, on day one they focused on *Use Your Word Wisely*. The tips included "speak possibility, keep your word and build trust, and avoid the downward spiral." To make the experience fun, each employee was given a bracelet. If one employee caught another employee in a downward-spiral conversation, he or she was authorized to take that person's bracelet. As you can imagine, people were really watching out for downward-spiral conversations and enjoying being extra careful to communicate impeccably. At the end of the day, those who had the most bracelets won prizes and were rewarded for wise use of their word.

Debbie, a graphic artist, says mastering the principle Use Your Word Wisely improved the quality of her work and home life: "I try to identify and avoid

Figure 17-1:

Customer Service Week at Modern Postcard

EXCELLENCE IN ACTION

CUSTOMER SERVICE WEEK
OCTOBER 3ʳᵈ – 7ᵀᴴ 2005

	Monday	Tuesday	Wednesday	Thursday	Friday
	3	4	5	6	7
Principle	Use Your Word Wisely	Be Accountable & Focus	Mine the Gold	Balance	Remember Rule #6
Action	Communicating with Quality and Integrity	Focusing on actively owning problems and striving to solve them	Bringing out the best in yourself and others	You are vital and energetic as a result of achieving a balanced life	Celebrate Excellence!
Events	Enjoy the Morning Bistro in each coffee bar Avoid the downward spiral for a chance to win a prize!	Ice Cream Social 2-3:00 p.m. in the Cafeteria Complete the Focus Search for more chances to win!	Jamba Juice 2-3:00 p.m. in the Cafeteria In Full Color Game-know your MP family for more chances to win! Your fortune by JTB	FREE massages from 1-4:00 p.m. Demonstrate your balancing skills for more chances to win BBQ on the Patio	Don't take yourself so seriously. Join us for Happy Hour and Hors D'oeuvres on the patio from 4-6:00 p.m. Music by "After Call"

downward-spiral conversations and/or turn them to a more positive subject. When I get stressed I try to put things in perspective and not take myself so seriously. I now leave work at work instead of taking work issues home with me."

Throughout Customer Service Week, employees were reminded of how they can be excellent in their business and personal lives. They were encouraged to take pride in their work and achievement and to compliment others on their good work, too. At the end of the week, the company celebrated with a nonalcoholic happy hour featuring catered food and an employee rock-and-roll band. The event allowed employees to bond, have some fun and celebrate their accomplishments.

Compensation at Modern Postcard is at market level, and yet employees express a high level of satisfaction. The leaders at the company have found ways to provide benefits to the employees that deliver the most bang for the buck. For instance, lunch in the company cafeteria is free. This saves employees money and encourages them to eat together, which builds camaraderie and creates more cohesiveness. The annual company picnic and lavish formal party provide additional opportunities for leadership to express appreciation and for employees to enjoy time together.

"We have a lot of Generation Y employees here, and it is really important for them to have a sense of connectedness and family involvement. For some of them, this may be their first or second job right out of college. They're looking to be in an organization where they feel part of a community. Relationships are important to them," Rodgers noted.

When employees have a social network at their workplace, they have more reasons to stay. By fostering a family-oriented environment, Modern Postcard offers an incentive for its employees to stay with the company over the long term.

"When we conduct exit interviews, the number one thing that people say is that they're going to miss the people," Rodgers said. "They always say, 'This is a great place to work.'"

Rodgers attributes the atmosphere of fun and joyfulness at Modern Postcard to co-founders Steve Hoffman, president and CEO, and Jim Toya-Brown, senior vice president.

"They are living examples of the principle 'Lighten Up,'" Rogers said. "They'll be the first ones to dress up in Halloween costumes or throw water balloons. They even accept a pie in the face good-naturedly. There's always something going on here. Steve and Jim always get involved, too."

Stephanie, a production supervisor, says remembering to lighten up was by far the most valuable principle for her: "I used to get so caught up in every little detail. I was so worried that any mistake would reflect poorly on me and my work ethic. You could say I was an expert at 'sweating the small stuff.' But this Excellence principle put every-thing into perspective for me. When I don't take myself so seriously, everything else is easier to deal with, and the small stuff just bounces off of me now!"

Recognition All Year Long

Modern Postcard takes advantage of Customer Service Week to promote excellence, but excellent behavior is recognized throughout the year, as well. On-the-spot awards of gift certificates or cash give managers the opportunity to reward employees who demonstrate excellence.

Image Awards are given quarterly to an individual in each department who has given excellent service either to customers or to fellow employees. The person receives a plaque and is recognized in a ceremony attended by the whole company.

Through various programs initiated by Modern Postcard's human resources depart-ment, the company has discovered a way to balance creativity with productivity. Like most companies its size, Modern Postcard offers benefits such as medical and dental coverage, 401(k) plans, profit sharing and paid time off. On top of this, Modern Postcard offers free lunch, on-site massage therapy, a mobile car wash, dry cleaning pick-up and delivery, annual celebrations and employee recognition programs.

Summing It Up

Excellence is a part of the mind-set at Modern Postcard. The Excellence principles have been incorporated into the orientation process and into customer-service training, and they are core competencies in the performance-review process.

Behind the postcards is a team of dedicated individuals who are motivated and enthusiastic about coming to work each day. Why? Because Modern Postcard has an absolute commitment to excellence in serving both customers and employees. While some companies sacrifice one for the other, Modern Postcard recognizes the impor-tance and value of both. That's why the company strives to create a dynamic environment in which its unique culture can grow and thrive.

In Chapter 4 we discussed the importance of cultivating the habit of excellence by following some practical strategies to implement the Excellence principles in your organi-zation. The following describes how Modern Postcard implemented those strategies:

* *Role Model Excellence*

Modern Postcard's senior management team, including the CEO, CFO and senior vice president, immersed themselves in the study of excellence by participating in a series of learning events and meetings. The focus of this first phase of Modern's Excellence initiative was to ensure leaders became strong role models of the principles by consistently integrating the concepts into their daily actions and behaviors.

- *Get Buy-In to Excellence*
  The next step was for management team members to enroll their direct reports in their vision for excellence. This involved sharing insights and successes with their direct report teams in regular staff meetings as well as highlighting the Excellence initiative in company communications.

- *Train Others in Excellence*
  Next, employees were given the opportunity to discover and master the six Excellence principles in a neutral environment. The program was facilitated by a certified Alliance for Organizational Excellence consultant. Groups of 25 to 30 employees participated in training sessions over a period of three to six months that were reinforced by activities and assignments based on real-world circumstances. A series of colorful postcard reminders for each of the Excellence principles was provided to participants as a means to deepen and reinforce their learning.

- *Implement Systems to Support Excellence*
  An Excellence Champion Group consisting of ambassadors from each department developed an Excellence strategy to implement new systems and processes that could create the context for sustained excellence.

- *Manage and Coach Excellence*
  Managers infused their daily management and coaching practices with the Excellence principles. They talked about excellence at every opportunity, including quarterly company updates, regular staff meetings, special events and one-on-one coaching meetings.

- *Acknowledge and Reward Excellence*
  Lastly, Modern Postcard acknowledged and rewarded demonstration of Excellence through its Customer Service Week celebrations and other spot awards.

Survey Results

You might be wondering how Modern Postcard's commitment to Excellence has paid off and what kinds of results have come about. Our data shows that up to 18 months after participating in the Excellence Program:

- 92 percent of respondents have applied the Excellence principles.
- 89 percent agree they are more effective.
- 81 percent agree the Excellence principles have helped them achieve better business results.
- 83 percent improved communication.

- 86 percent are more accountable.
- 81 percent are more focused.
- 81 percent improved interpersonal relationships with internal and external customers.
- 72 percent are more engaged.

How does this translate into the bottom line? Modern Postcard achieved unprecedented growth and increased revenue in 2005—with the third quarter its best quarter in history (the highest average-order value). Although daily job volume increased, turnaround time decreased by 64 percent, customer service satisfaction increased to 92 percent and overall employee satisfaction is at 85 percent. Employee retention is consistently high. The company received the Crystal Award at the San Diego Society for Human Resource Management Workplace Excellence Awards in November 2005 for its demonstration of human resources practices that contribute to superior employee and company performance.

Winning the Workplace Excellence Award has been an effective tool for Modern Postcard to use to attract top talent. The company's job-opening Web page and recruitment advertising includes mention of this award having drawn a record number of qualified candidates and having persuaded highly desirable talent to choose Modern Postcard. For example, Blake Miller, vice president of sales and marketing, previously a senior executive with Hewlett-Packard, where he spear-headed the development of the all-in-one printer, fax and scanner, chose Modern Postcard over big-name companies like Dell.

Employees at Modern Postcard report improved engagement, communication and accountability as well as increased productivity. Jason works in the press department and faces intense demand every day. In the past, he felt fragmented and frustrated by the overwhelming workload. Now he believes that he understands more of what it takes to do more. He says, "The focus is in me. I can't change anyone; I can only do what I do the best that I can do it. Therefore, I have been able to focus on my responsibilities and thus I am outputting more work." Jason is not the only employee at Modern Postcard who feels he is more productive. Seventy-five percent of participants feel that they are making better use of their time and energy and that they have improved productivity as a result of application of the Excellence principles. Their productivity responses were as follows:

- 22 percent report their productivity has improved about 10 percent.
- 33 percent report their productivity has improved about 20 percent.
- 6 percent report their productivity has improved about 30 percent.
- 6 percent report their productivity has improved about 40 percent.

chapter 18

Padre Dam Municipal Water District: Excellence in Government

So far we have looked mainly at corporations, but excellence is possible to achieve in any organization—even government. One public service agency that has been able to successfully operationalize the Excellence principles is Padre Dam Municipal Water District. Padre Dam is a very unusual organization, unusual in that it's a public agency with a private sector mind-set. Employees at every level of the organization, including the blue-collar workers who dig the ditches and fix the sewerage leaks, are considered leaders, and are treated as such.

Padre Dam's mission is "to provide quality water, recycled water, park and recreational facilities and wastewater-management services for customers in the most cost-effective manner possible, earning customer and community respect."

Padre Dam's journey to excellence began in 1996, when August Caires became general manager. At the time, there were a number of disgruntled employees and acrimonious relationships; there had even been a few lawsuits directed at the utility by former employees. Change was critical.

In 1997, the utility initiated a Workforce Partnership, establishing labor, management and the board of directors as equal partners in problem solving, decision-making, strategic planning, employee empowerment and development, and organizational communications. The culture changed radically as employees became invested in the future of the utility.

"Employees are our most valued asset," Caires said. "Individual success equals a broader success. Our Workforce Partnership empowers employees in the decision-making process."

The utility's continuing goal is to develop a customer-focused and employee-driven organization built on the core values of trust, integrity, competence, accountability and service.

Augie, as Caires prefers to be known, is the quintessential enlightened leader. At his retirement party, his management team, staff and business partners all affirmed the high level of integrity he brought to his work. In every way, he could be counted on to be a powerful role model of excellence and to do the right thing in the right way. He is a leader with great vision, courage and authenticity, as well as being highly service-oriented. Although Augie requested he be "roasted" at his retirement celebration, the audience had difficulty coming up with any shortcomings.

In 2002, Caires was selected as one of the Top 10 Public Works Leaders of the Year, and Padre Dam won the Workplace Excellence Award from the Society for Human Resource Management. The Workplace Excellence Awards recognize organizations whose human resources programs have a positive impact on business performance.

Reigniting the Passion

As new employees came on board, some of the original excitement about the Workplace Partnership dissipated, and as Debi Groat-Baczynski, director of human resources, notes, the workforce had become complacent.

"We needed to raise the bar," she said. "We needed to be reminded of what we were all about."

Every two years the management team at Padre Dam conducts an assessment and direction workshop, looking closely at the culture of the organization to determine where it wants to go next and how to get there. In an effort to reinvigorate the workforce and breathe new life into the core concepts, Padre Dam leadership adopted the Excellence principles and made the Excellence program available to all employees. Three sessions were conducted, with 25 people in each session.

"Our goal is to be an employer of choice," Baczynski said. Hired in 1991 as Padre Dam's first director of human resources, Baczynski upgraded recruiting, hiring, training and benefits programs at Padre Dam. When she learned about the Excellence program, she realized it would take her team and the rest of the utility to the next level. "We felt this training would enable our employees to be better employees and to enrich their own lives at the same time."

The upper-level executives and the entire management team participated in the program. The concepts meshed well with the overall philosophy of the organization and gave management a framework into which it could integrate excellence into the utility's operations. Department heads now use the concepts in their meetings and ask for feedback from their direct reports. The customer-service department keeps laminated cards that display the principles and use them as reminders about how they want to perform their jobs.

"These are simple concepts," Baczynski said, "which makes them very useful. I have gotten very positive feedback, and I hear people use the terminology in their discussions. The concepts are easy to remember and easy to retain. People have told me they found the concepts were also helpful at home when dealing with a spouse or children."

One of the major benefits that Padre Dam has seen since implementing the principles is improved communication. Employees are much more aware of the downward spiral and of how they are using their words.

In fact, one employee wrote in the post-program survey, "I waste very little time these days discussing the negatives of other people's work habits and their reluctance to change. This gives me more time to help the people who are positive and willing to learn and/or make changes."

For many people, the principles correlate with their personal values.

Another participant said, "The Principles are good reminders to me. I keep the cards on the desk. I have my vision statement on the desk. I try to remember not to get entangled in the negative conversations, and I always try to give positive feedback and keep others' buckets full by giving them positive feedback."

For others, the principles are a reminder to stay positive. One said, "Cynical behavior is common in public agencies, and the basic Principles of Excellence remind me to continue to take an active, positive stance on a daily basis and to develop a reputation of integrity and fairness."

In the case of a utility team, the principles motivated its members to be more customer-focused. John, the supervisor, tells the story of how he and his team treated a customer with particular kindness and respect. "We were out digging up some pipes and had cordoned off the street. An elderly lady was having difficulty driving around the safety cones and, in her frustration, began cussing at us for blocking the road with our service vehicles. In the past, we would have snickered and ignored her, allowing her to struggle. But, since participating in the Excellence program, this kind of behavior no longer feels right. I went over to her car, apologized for the inconvenience and guided her through the cones so she could be on her way. She thanked us, and it felt good to know we had represented the water district in the best way."

Because workers from all levels of the organization received training in Excellence, the principles have become embedded in the interrelationships between management and frontline workers.

"The teaching starts at the top and flows down to the employees, but then they push the teaching back up. It comes from both directions," Baczynski says. She notes that talking about excellence and the principles as much as possible helps ingrain them into the culture so that they become part of each person's lifestyle. "We have a collaborative workforce. Employees don't hesitate to remind even management of the concepts. It's been easy to make it a part of our ongoing culture."

Excellence is Not a Fair-Weather Concept

Every organization faces challenges, and Padre Dam Municipal Water District is no different. When major transitions occur, it is important for leaders and their employees to have a foundational philosophy to help them weather the storms.

When Padre Dam was under threat of privatization recently, its leaders employed the Excellence principles to keep everyone focused. Everyone in the organization agreed to the principles by signing a poster displaying the principles that was then framed and hung in the lobby as a reminder.

The privatization challenge was overcome, and the next challenge facing the organization involved retirements at the top levels and financial constraints from the board of directors.

"When we started talking about all the positive things in the situation, we realized we were in a better position than we thought," Baczynski observed. "The employees were staying positive, being the best employees and the best in customer service in spite of everything else."

While dealing with challenging situations, the management at Padre Dam has made it a priority to be transparent throughout the organization.

"The employees know that they can ask us anything and they'll get the same story from whomever they speak to, along with the documentation and evidence to back it up. We're not going to make the situation worse or better than it is. This really helps keep the trust level high," Baczynski said.

In keeping with its philosophy, the management at Padre Dam is looking toward the future and continuing to look for ways to change and improve.

"We don't believe in 'business as usual' just because we're a public agency. We have no intention of maintaining the status quo," Baczynski concluded.

Excellence in Action

Suzie, an employee at Padre Dam, took the Excellence principles to heart and religiously incorporated them into her work. The result for her was a promotion to the position of information system specialist. Doug Wilson, director of finance, wrote the following: "Suzie successfully competed for this appointment against five outside candidates who were also well qualified. Her past excellent performance in prior positions helped support her bid for this job."

Suzie's promotion was a direct result of her successful application of Excellence principles and her commitment to leadership. In a memo to her fellow employees, Suzie sent a special thanks to members of her Excellence team. In her memo, she wrote: "I appreciate the time and effort you have put into polishing this gold flake. I feel very shiny right now."

chapter 19

The Excellence Game

Mitchell International is a software solutions and ASP provider that relies on highly skilled knowledge workers. The Information Systems (IS) department introduced the Excellence program as a means to keep employees focused on priorities, to establish a positive work environment and to restore trust and confidence in times of change.

While the average turnover in the industry is 11 percent, Mitchell's IS department successfully limited turnover to 5 percent in 2005, a 3-percent decrease from 2004. Vice President of IS Linda Amaro attributes increased retention and improved morale to continued reinforcement and integration of the Excellence principles.

"Using the principles got us back on track through a lot of changes, including Y2K, management changes and switching from print to software," Amaro says. "At first the chaos was almost beyond what the team could handle, but the Excellence principles allowed the team to focus on priorities. We established new rules of engagement. It takes a conscious effort to use the principles, but eventually it becomes automatic."

One of the methods that Mitchell International has developed for integrating the Excellence principles into the workplace is the Mitchellopoly Game, a game based on the Excellence principles that was created by a group of engineers in the IS department.

The poster-size laminated board with colorful graphics is wall-mounted for display during the week and taken down for the weekly Excellence game. A series of recognition cards reflecting each of the Excellence principles is turned in for a chance to roll the dice. Here is a simplified explanation of how the game works:

- Any employee may award an Excellence Recognition Card to any other employee (including management) to recognize that person for demonstrating one of the Excellence principles. The award cards may be turned in every week for a monthly drawing ticket and a roll of the dice to play the game and move around the board.

- For every award card received, the player receives one roll and a ticket.
- For each roll of the dice, the person is allowed to move the number of spaces that appears on the dice. There are several Opportunity spaces they draw from the stack of Opportunity Cards. They can win prizes, "Get out of Lockup" cards or move-ahead cards, or move to "GO."
- Every time players pass GO, they are awarded another ticket for the monthly drawing, and they may select a prize from the gift basket.

The game is a way to bring fun into the workplace and to promote excellent behavior at the same time. For instance, if a player lands on Excellence Lockup, the player is stuck there until awarded a Get Out of Lockup card. This is achieved either by Hard Labor (running the weekly game), Time Off for Good Behavior (working beyond the normal schedule) or attending an Excellence Lockup Breakfast, which is bimonthly and includes discussions about how to get others involved in the program or how employees can work better together. When they land in Lockup, they are, in effect, rewarded with a breakfast with the vice president.

To keep everyone involved, a status sheet of the weekly game highlights is sent out to employees that includes who is in the lead, who is new to the game, funny things that happened and who landed in Lockup. The list also includes all of the players in order to show the standings and number of people involved.

Of course, rewards are an important part of the game. A drawing is held at a Monthly All-Hands Meeting in which news is communicated and the Excellence principles are reinforced. Prizes usually include gift cards to local eateries and coffee shops or gift baskets filled with goodies.

Leadership at Mitchell will tell you that the game is infectious. Some employees collect the cards and hang them in their cubicle as badges of honor. And when high-level engineering directors show up in the cafeteria Thursdays at noon to play a game, other people in the cafeteria come and watch to join in on the fun.

Darlene, a principal database administrator, reported that the game was a success in boosting morale. "Sometimes peer review speaks volumes, and these Excellence Cards have been just the 'pat on the back' that the staff needs from their peers to reignite motivation during a challenging week or any given day or project, for that matter. As we lose energy we expend toward the job, the card serves as appreciation and (having it) delivered by a team member really seems to have a 'special' meaning as compared to recognition by your boss."

According to Amaro, the emphasis on excellence differentiates Mitchell from many other companies, and the cards help keep the concept alive. When she catches people being excellent, she attaches a sheet of paper to the recognition card that lists the Excellence principles so they get an Excellence refresher at the same time they see how their action pertained to that principle.

Not only does the receiver of the card receive a morale boost, but those who deliver the cards report an "uplifting feeling."

Since operationalizing the Excellence principles, Amaro said, "I have seen a difference in behavior, stronger teams and commitment to do the job with quality."

chapter 20

Conclusion

"There is no passion to be found playing small—in settling for a life that is less than the one you are capable of living."

—Nelson Mandela

When we look at the winners in the real-life game of excellence that we have considered in the previous several chapters, we can see certain commonalities. Each organization puts a high premium on values. The companies are known for being flexible, innovative and people-oriented. They provide a structure for individual creative enterprise and reward behavior that is in alignment with the organizational mission. Their leaders are role models of excellence who are willing to evolve and continually respond to a changing world.

Excellence for the winners is a strategically planned outcome. It doesn't happen by accident or by luck, which is good news. This means that excellence can be achieved by any organization willing to put excellence in the forefront of its activities. The tools to achieve excellence are available, and examples of excellence abound. The purpose of this book was to get you started on the path to excellence. When the principles are embedded and become "business as usual" at your organization, you will have the foundation you need to institute change and create an environment of passion, creativity, innovation, integrity and continued excellence.

You may believe that such a level of excellence would never be possible in your particular company because you believe that the executive team will never get on board. It's true that the ideal situation for implementing excellence begins at the executive level, but in reality, excellence can be brought into the culture at any access point—whether at the grassroots level, the middle-management level or the executive level.

If a culture of excellence is instituted at one of the lower levels, the pressure and momentum usually forces the executives to get on board. This is not to say that it embarrasses any individual or group into behaving a certain way. Instead, it affects the entire organization in subtle and yet recognizable ways that, over time, will create a culture of excellence.

Although a culture of excellence cannot be imposed on people, if you give people tools and strategies to communicate at the highest level of excellence, they will find it is actually easier and takes less energy and thought to be open, kind and respectful than it does to be closed, mean and withholding. Excellence is a learning and discovering process that can take anywhere from three months to a year, but if you are committed to the change, you will begin to see results. You will feel more passion for your work, and you will see that passion reflected in those around you.

Excellence (or success) is not identifying how others aren't excelling. Sometimes we fall into the trap of thinking that our state of excellence, as an individual or organization, is determined by our ability to clearly identify, and point out, where others are not excelling. We are so programmed to look outside of ourselves for reference on how well we are doing that we mistakenly think that the degree to which we are excelling is in direct proportion to the degree to which others aren't excelling.

Excellence has nothing at all to do with comparing or competing. It is about our willingness to keep seeing ourselves in new ways, to keep challenging our edges, to keep looking for ways to move forward in the most powerful and inspiring way— not because we have to or because if we don't we will suffer, but because we are committed to excellence in the most radical way.

Excellence in the Talent Age

The concept of excellence is intertwined with the idea of talent. Excellence fosters, attracts and elicits talent. Thomas Friedman, *New York Times* columnist and acclaimed author of *The World is Flat*, has described the early 21st century as the dawning of the "Talent Age." He wrote, "It's just not so much what you know; it's how you learn, because what you know today will likely be outdated sooner in a flat world."

Friedman goes on to say that the Talent Age is a result of the information revolution and the "flattening of the world." Because we can now access human talent anywhere—whether it's in India for services or China for manufacturing or the United States for innovation—the kind of talent your organization can attract and utilize is really what management consultants John Seeley Brown and John Hagel called "the only sustainable edge."

So we're now in an age in which leaders must look to strengthen and aggregate more human talent, more human capital. According to Friedman, "Talent is the differentiator beyond cost." In other words, those who are looking for certain goods and services are going to look beyond the cost to the talent that your organization offers. Friedman defines talent as "the ability to imagine and synthesize different products or value opportunities and then to execute them, to design them, to refine them."

And the kind of environment required for this sort of creative and innovative work is an environment in which people are focused, joyful and operating at their full potential.

How You Can Use the Excellence Principles

First, begin to apply the principles to every aspect of your life. "Excellence," as you may know, is an absolute word. You can't be very excellent or sort of excellent. You are either excellent or you're not.

Next, find some like-minded individuals in your workplace and form a study group based on this book and the Excellence principles. Hold each other up to the high standards exemplified by the principles. Encourage your board of directors to read this book and to hold themselves to a high standard. Begin to implement *Principle #6 -Lighten Up* in the workplace, and when people wonder what you're up to, recommend that they learn and use the principles.

Let the underlying ethos of your workplace be about each person living up to his or her fullest potential and helping others to live up to their fullest potential for the greatest good of the company.

Think about this: do you reward competitive or cooperative behavior? Just think if all your sales teams shared information rather than hoarding it to try to beat the others. Oprah Winfrey throws a party for her entire organization—and it's a doozy. Once she took all of them to Hawaii. Now you may not want to take your entire company to Hawaii, but have you thought about rewards and incentives for production and for entire teams or departments based on their productivity and results?

In the TV reality show "Survivor," only one person at the end of the show is the survivor. He or she has to be cutthroat and competitive. But for civilization to survive, people have to help each other. They have to be cooperative.

Start with Intention

The first step in achieving excellence is to make an intention to be excellent. You align your values with the Excellence principles. You learn the "symptoms" of excellence. You bring these principles to your awareness with every possible interaction. Next, you introduce the concepts to managers. You ask them to make an intention to be excellent. You ask them to be clear about the values and to be on the lookout for symptoms of excellence. You find ways to keep the principles at the forefront of their attention. Finally, the entire workforce is introduced to the principles. They understand that it is the goal of the company to be excellent in all ways, including in the treatment of employees. They understand that to be in sync with the company they must begin to adopt the principles and adapt them to their situations. They must realize that the bar is set high and that if they want to stay with the company and advance, they must use the principles so that they can meet the challenges and also reap the rewards—meaningful employment and a more joy-filled life.

Ralph Marston, author of the online "Daily Motivator," wrote: "With your thoughts, your actions, your attitude and your spirit, you can make the world a better place, every day, in every situation. Get in the habit of doing just that, and you'll savor the rich rewards." If you make excellence a part of your life through your thoughts, actions, attitude and spirit, then you will be doing exactly what Marston describes. Not only will your work life and your personal life improve immensely, but you will also be making the world a better place.

Appendix:
Action Pages and Success Logs

Excellence Implementation Plan

Excellence demands adaptability, imagination and vigor, but most of all it requires a constant state of self-discovery and discipline. You may find it easy to go back to conducting "business as usual"—doing the same old things that guarantee you stay stuck, or at a minimum miss your mark. To successfully master the Excellence principles, you will need to immerse yourself in studying, understanding and practicing them.

In Part Two of this book, you completed an Action Plan for each principle. As discussed previously, I recommend that you form an Excellence Champion Group and use the worksheets in the implementation plan to create broader enterprise-wide change. At the end of each section, meet with your Excellence Champion Group to report on your successes and challenges. Your Excellence Champion Group will be a powerful source of support and reinforcement. Set specific, regular times at which you will speak and hold each other accountable for increasing excellence.

My Excellence Champion Group

	Name	E-mail	Phone
1.			
2.			
3.			
4.			

Champion-Group Meeting Times

	Date	Time	Place
1.			
2.			
3.			
4.			

How will you hold yourself and your Champion Group accountable for excellence?

_____

_____

_____

_____

1 Use Your Word Wisely - Worksheet

Committing to Excellence

What are your goals for communication in your organization?

Implementing Systems

What new systems, processes or structures will you implement to promote improved communication?

Taking Action

What specific actions will you take to implement these new systems? When?

Measuring Progress

What specific behaviors and results would you need to see in order to feel that progress has been made?

Holding Firm

It is easy to slip into old patterns. List the factors (triggers) that might cause people to slip back (e.g., stress, fatigue, time pressures) and the strategies you will use to help people hold firm in their new behaviors.

_____

_____

_____

_____

Success Log

It's common for people to overlook the progress they've made. Make a point of looking for and acknowledging increased awareness; conversations about what's possible; reductions in criticism, complaints and condemnation; and any incident that demonstrates improved quality of communication in your organization.

1. _____

2. _____

3. _____

4. _____

5. _____

6. _____

7. _____

8. _____

9. _____

10. _____

#2 Be Accountable – Worksheet

Committing to Excellence
What are your goals for accountability in your organization?

_____

_____

_____

_____

Implementing Systems
What new systems, processes or structures will you implement to promote increased accountability?

_____

_____

_____

_____

Taking Action
What specific actions will you take to implement these new systems? When?

_____

_____

_____

_____

Measuring Progress
What specific behaviors and results would you need to see in order to feel that progress has been made?

_____

_____

_____

_____

Holding Firm

It is easy to slip into old patterns. List the factors (triggers) that might cause people to slip back (e.g., stress, fatigue, time pressures) and the strategies you will use to help people hold firm in their new behaviors.

_____

_____

_____

_____

Success Log

It's common for people to overlook the progress they've made. Make a point of looking for and acknowledging increased awareness; increased accountable behaviors; efforts to be proactive; improved collaboration; and any incident that demonstrates increased accountability in your organization.

1. _____

2. _____

3. _____

4. _____

5. _____

6. _____

7. _____

8. _____

9. _____

10. _____

#3 Focus – Worksheet

Committing to Excellence

What are your goals for focus in your organization?

_____

_____

_____

_____

Implementing Systems

What new systems, processes or structures will you implement to promote increased focus?

_____

_____

_____

_____

Taking Action

What specific actions will you take to implement these new systems? When?

_____

_____

_____

_____

Measuring Progress

What specific behaviors and results would you need to see in order to feel that progress has been made?

_____

_____

_____

_____

Holding Firm

It is easy to slip into old patterns. List the factors (triggers) that might cause people to slip back (e.g., stress, fatigue, time pressures) and the strategies you will use to help people hold firm in their new behaviors.

_____

_____

_____

_____

Success Log

It's common for people to overlook the progress they've made. Make a point of looking for and acknowledging more efficient use of time and energy; elimination of distractions; increased presence; and any incident that demonstrates sharper focus and greater alignment in your organization.

1. _____

2. _____

3. _____

4. _____

5. _____

6. _____

7. _____

8. _____

9. _____

10. _____

#4 Mine the Gold – Worksheet

Committing to Excellence
What are your goals for interpersonal relationships in your organization?

_____

_____

_____

_____

Implementing Systems
What new systems, processes or structures will you implement to promote improved relationships?

_____

_____

_____

_____

Taking Action
What specific actions will you take to implement these new systems? When?

_____

_____

_____

_____

Measuring Progress
What specific behaviors and results would you need to see in order to feel that progress has been made?

_____

_____

_____

_____

Holding Firm

It is easy to slip into old patterns. List the factors (triggers) that might cause people to slip back (e.g., stress, fatigue, time pressures) and the strategies you will use to help people hold firm in their new behaviors.

_____

_____

_____

_____

Success Log

It's common for people to overlook the progress they've made. Make a point of looking for and acknowledging increased respect; better utilization of talent and skill; more frequent acknowledgment of others' contributions; and any incident that demonstrates improved relationships in your organization.

1. _____

2. _____

3. _____

4. _____

5. _____

6. _____

7. _____

8. _____

9. _____

10. _____

5 Strive for Balance – Worksheet

Committing to Excellence
What are your goals for balance in your organization?

_____

_____

_____

_____

Implementing Systems
What new systems, processes or structures will you implement to promote improved balance?

_____

_____

_____

_____

Taking Action
What specific actions will you take to implement these new systems? When?

_____

_____

_____

_____

Measuring Progress
What specific behaviors and results would you need to see in order to feel that progress has been made?

_____

_____

_____

_____

Holding Firm

It is easy to slip into old patterns. List the factors (triggers) that might cause people to slip back (e.g., stress, fatigue, time pressures) and the strategies you will use to help people hold firm in their new behaviors.

_____

_____

_____

_____

Success Log

It's common for people to overlook the progress they've made. Make a point of looking for and acknowledging more effective management of personal energy; healthier habits; greater commitment to seeking balance; and any incident that demonstrates increased energy and vitality in your organization.

1. _____

2. _____

3. _____

4. _____

5. _____

6. _____

7. _____

8. _____

9. _____

10. _____

#6 Lighten Up – Worksheet

Committing to Excellence

What are your goals for fun and enjoyment in your organization?

Implementing Systems

What new systems will you implement to create a more enjoyable work environment?

Taking Action

What specific actions will you take to implement these new systems? When?

Measuring Progress

What specific behaviors and results would you need to see in order to feel that progress has been made?

Holding Firm

It is easy to slip into old patterns. List the factors (triggers) that might cause people to slip back (e.g., stress, fatigue, time pressures) and the strategies you will use to help people hold firm in their new behaviors.

_____

_____

_____

_____

Success Log

It's common for people to overlook the progress they've made. Make a point of looking for and acknowledging improved attitude; efforts to bring appropriate humor to the workplace; and any incident that serves to create a more enjoyable work environment.

1. _____

2. _____

3. _____

4. _____

5. _____

6. _____

7. _____

8. _____

9. _____

10. _____

Measuring Excellence

As you implement systems and processes to increase excellence in your organization, you will want to measure progress and positive change. The following are some ways in which you might apply metrics to your initiatives:

_____ % retention of top performers

_____ % employee engagement

_____ % reduction of employee-relations incidents

_____ % reduction of labor-related legal action

_____ % customer satisfaction

_____ % retention of solid performers

_____ % of employees who meet or exceed cultural competencies on annual performance review

_____ % of employees who agree senior leaders are excellent role models of your culture

_____ % of employees who refer a qualified job candidate

_____ % of employees who refer to your company as a great place to work

_____ % of top candidates who seek a position in your company

_____ % of top candidates who accept a position in your company

_____ % of employees who are involved in training and development activities

_____ % of employees who are considered for promotions

_____ % of bad hires who terminate or quit within 12 months

_____ % of employees who cite the work environment or relationship with direct manager as a primary reason for quitting

_____ number of workplace-excellence awards/recognition

Operational measures:

_____ (time) it takes on average to resolve a typical problem

_____ (time) it takes on average to reach a typical decision

_____ (time) it takes to complete new-customer installation

_____ (time) it takes to respond to a typical customer concern

_____ (time) it takes on average to resolve a typical customer complaint

_____ (number) of levels or people a problem is referred to before final resolution is made

_____ Number of hours/days spent on typical staff conflict or human-resources issues

_____ Average attendance rate (include sick days, personal days, etc.)

_____ Average attrition (resignations, terminations, layoffs, etc)

_____ Average number and frequency of employee-relations issues (include legal action)

_____ (number) of employees identified for development or skill advancement

Excellent Workplace Assessment

This assessment is intended to help you take a high-level view of your company's culture, management, leadership, people processes and environment—key elements of an employer-of-choice organization. From this perspective you will be able to determine where your strengths are and where you need to improve in order to build an "Excellent Workplace."

Establish a Culture of Excellence

1. Communication: *(Use Your Word Wisely)*
What is the quality of communication in your company?

LEVEL ONE	LEVEL TWO	LEVEL THREE	LEVEL FOUR
Entry Level	Developing	Acceptable Standard	Employer of Choice
The quality of communication is poor.	Company aware of need to improve standard of communication.	Company initiatives focus on improving communication.	Communication is impeccable.
1.	2.	3.	4.

2. Accountability *(Be Accountable)*
How accountable are people in your company?

LEVEL ONE	LEVEL TWO	LEVEL THREE	LEVEL FOUR
Entry Level	Developing	Acceptable Standard	Employer of Choice
There is little accountability.	Company aware of need to increase accountability.	Company initiatives drive increased accountability.	Level of accountability is high.
1.	2.	3.	4.

3. Alignment *(Focus)*
How aligned are people, teams and departments with business?

LEVEL ONE	LEVEL TWO	LEVEL THREE	LEVEL FOUR
Entry Level	Developing	Acceptable Standard	Employer of Choice
There is little alignment.	Company aware of need to increase alignment.	Company initiatives drive increased alignment.	Degree of alignment is high.
1.	2.	3.	4.

4. Relationships: *(Mine the Gold)*

What is the quality of relationships in your company?

LEVEL ONE	LEVEL TWO	LEVEL THREE	LEVEL FOUR
Entry Level	Developing	Acceptable Standard	Employer of Choice
The quality of relationships is poor.	Company aware of need to improve relationships.	Company initiatives focus on improving relationships.	Relationships are collaborative and talent is maximized.
1.	2.	3.	4.

5. Energy: *(Strive for Balance)*

What is the level of energy in your company?

LEVEL ONE	LEVEL TWO	LEVEL THREE	LEVEL FOUR
Entry Level	Developing	Acceptable Standard	Employer of Choice
Energy is low.	Company aware of need to improve balance and increase energy.	Company initiatives support work-life balance.	There is good work-life balance and high levels of energy.
1.	2.	3.	4.

6. Fun: *(Lighten Up)*

Do people enjoy work and thrive in your company?

LEVEL ONE	LEVEL TWO	LEVEL THREE	LEVEL FOUR
Entry Level	Developing	Acceptable Standard	Employer of Choice
There is little joy and fulfillment.	Company aware of need to improve the work environment.	Company initiatives support work-life balance.	People are thriving and love coming to work.
1.	2.	3.	4.

Develop Excellent Managers

1. Attract:

How well do your managers attract, seek and scout for top talent?

LEVEL ONE Entry Level	LEVEL TWO Developing	LEVEL THREE Acceptable Standard	LEVEL FOUR Employer of Choice
Managers are not expected to attract talent.	Company aware managers are key to attracting talent.	Company initiatives focus on attracting talent.	Managers are expert at attracting talent.
1.	2.	3.	4.

2. Optimize:

How well do your managers optimize talent and build strong relationships?

LEVEL ONE Entry Level	LEVEL TWO Developing	LEVEL THREE Acceptable Standard	LEVEL FOUR Employer of Choice
Talent is unrealized and relationships are tenuous.	Company aware of need to optimize talent and strengthen relationships.	Company initiatives drive talent optimization and relationships.	Talent is fully optimized and relationships are strong.
1.	2.	3.	4.

3. Retain:

How well do your managers inspire and influence employees to stay?

LEVEL ONE Entry Level	LEVEL TWO Developing	LEVEL THREE Acceptable Standard	LEVEL FOUR Employer of Choice
Turnover is prevalent.	Company aware of need to increase retention.	Company initiatives drive increased retention.	Retention is high. Top talent stays.
1.	2.	3.	4.

Enlighten Leaders

1. Role Model Excellence

How well do your leaders role model Excellence?

LEVEL ONE	LEVEL TWO	LEVEL THREE	LEVEL FOUR
Entry Level	Developing	Acceptable Standard	Employer of Choice
Leaders are weak role models of Excellence.	Leaders aware of need to be stronger role models.	Leaders are engaged in initiatives to be strong role models.	Leaders are role models of Excellence.
1.	2.	3.	4.

2. Inspire trust and respect

How well do your leaders inspire trust and respect, and provide strong direction?

LEVEL ONE	LEVEL TWO	LEVEL THREE	LEVEL FOUR
Entry Level	Developing	Acceptable Standard	Employer of Choice
Leaders are not trusted and respected to provide direction.	Leaders aware of need to inspire trust and respect, and strong direction.	Leadership initiatives drive trust and respect, and clear direction.	Leaders inspire trust and respect, and provide strong direction.
1.	2.	3.	4.

3. Mastery of high-level leadership competencies.

Are your leaders courageous, authentic, service-oriented, truthful and effective?

LEVEL ONE	LEVEL TWO	LEVEL THREE	LEVEL FOUR
Entry Level	Developing	Acceptable Standard	Employer of Choice
Leaders do not exhibit high-level leadership competencies.	Leaders aware of need to increase leadership competency.	Initiatives drive leadership mastery.	Leaders have achieved mastery of high-level competencies.
1.	2.	3.	4.

Align People Processes

1. Talent Management

To what degree do your people processes help you to attract, optimize and retain top talent?

LEVEL ONE	LEVEL TWO	LEVEL THREE	LEVEL FOUR
Entry Level	Developing	Acceptable Standard	Employer of Choice
People processes do not attract top talent, optimize performance or promote retention.	Company aware of need to adjust processes to enable more effective talent management.	Company initiatives focus on making processes more attractive.	People processes attract top talent, optimize performance and promote retention.
1.	2.	3.	4.

2. Build Trust and Respect

To what degree do your people processes build trust and respect?

LEVEL ONE	LEVEL TWO	LEVEL THREE	LEVEL FOUR
Entry Level	Developing	Acceptable Standard	Employer of Choice
People processes do not build trust and respect.	Company aware of need to adjust processes to build trust and respect.	Initiatives focus on adjusting processes to build trust and respect.	People processes build trust and respect.
1.	2.	3.	4.

3. Reward Desired Behaviors

To what degree do your people processes reward desired behaviors?

LEVEL ONE	LEVEL TWO	LEVEL THREE	LEVEL FOUR
Entry Level	Developing	Acceptable Standard	Employer of Choice
People processes do not reward desired behaviors.	Company aware of need to adjust processes to reward desired behaviors.	Initiatives focus on adjusting processes to reward desired behaviors.	People processes reward desired behaviors.
1.	2.	3.	4.

4. Reflect and Reinforce the Excellence Principles

To what degree do your people processes reflect and reinforce the Excellence principles?

LEVEL ONE	LEVEL TWO	LEVEL THREE	LEVEL FOUR
Entry Level	Developing	Acceptable Standard	Employer of Choice
Processes do not reflect and reinforce Excellence principles.	Company aware of need to adjust processes to reinforce Excellence.	Initiatives focus on adjusting processes to reinforce Excellence principles.	People processes reflect and reinforce Excellence principles.
1.	2.	3.	4.

Create Value

1. Pride, meaning and belonging
Does your work environment promote pride, meaning and a sense of belonging?

LEVEL ONE	LEVEL TWO	LEVEL THREE	LEVEL FOUR
Entry Level	Developing	Acceptable Standard	Employer of Choice
Environment does not promote pride, meaning and belonging.	Company aware of need to offer opportunities to increase pride, meaning and belonging.	Initiatives focus on creating an environment of pride, meaning and belonging.	Work environment promotes pride, meaning and a strong sense of belonging.
1.	2.	3.	4.

2. Recognition and reputation
Has your company been recognized as a top employer, and have you built a reputation as a great place to work?

LEVEL ONE	LEVEL TWO	LEVEL THREE	LEVEL FOUR
Entry Level	Developing	Acceptable Standard	Employer of Choice
Company is not recognized as a great place to work.	Company aware of need to gain recognition and build a reputation as a great place to work.	Initiatives focus on gaining recognition and building a reputation as a great place to work.	Company is recognized as a top employer and has a reputation as a great place to work.
1.	2.	3.	4.

Excellence Resources

Excellence Learning and Consulting Programs
On-site Excellence Programs combine high-content, high-participation classroom learning with real-world application, powerful coaching and strategic consulting to help you achieve better business results.

Excellence Recognition Cards
Reinforce, recognize and reward your employees with Excellence Recognition Cards. Vibrant, four-color, standard-size postcards of each of the six Excellence principles feature distinctive images on the front and note space on the back for managers or peers to write a personal message to the employee being recognized. Insert your company's logo, vision and values for a custom look and feel.

Excellence Video
Excellence for Life: Ideas to Challenge and Inspire You to Be Your Best provides an innovative way to begin or end any meeting by focusing participants on the key elements of excellence. DVD format.

The Excellence Game™
This interactive training game includes real-world case studies, team activities and stimulating discussion that helps you to learn and apply the Excellence principles. Groups of two to six players explore workplace challenges and gain new tools for improving communication, increasing accountability, sharpening focus, enhancing interpersonal relationships, and bringing more energy and passion to their work. When players have completed the six lessons, they graduate to the Excellence Mastery round, in which they compete for recognition and reward of personal and professional excellence.

Management 2010 Dashboard™
Our exclusive Management 2010 Dashboard™ reinforces and rewards your managers' talent management efforts on 15 key indicators showing monthly progress and comparison charts, offering a unique feature to help you link your talent-management initiatives to bottom-line business results.

Excellence Engagement Index™
Measure employee engagement quickly, easily and economically with the

Excellence Engagement Index™. This practical online tool gives you critical information about the number of employees who are engaged, "coasting" and "checking out" so that your managers can take immediate action to remove barriers and optimize employee performance.

Visit http://www.uexcel.com for more information.

Bibliography

Ahlrichs, Nancy. 2003. *Manager of Choice: Five Competencies for Cultivating Top Talent*. Mountain View: Davies-Black Publishing.

Barrett, Richard. 2005. "Cultural Capital: The New Frontier of Competitive Advantage; Increasing Market Value by Leveraging the Intangibles." *The Values Center*: www.valuescenter.com

Canfield, Jack; Hansen, Mark Victor; Hewitt, Les. 2000. *The Power of Focus: How to Hit Your Business, Personal and Financial Targets with Absolute Certainty*. Deerfield Beach: Health Communications.

Carlson, Richard. 1997. *Don't Sweat the Small Stuff*. New York: Hyperion.

Connors, Roger; Smith, Tom; Hickman, Craig. 1994. *The Oz Principle*. Paramus: Prentice-Hall Press.

Cooper, Robert K. 2001. *The Other 90%: How to Unlock Your Vast Untapped Potential for Leadership & Life*. New York: Crown Business.

Corporate Executive Board. 2004. *Driving Performance and Retention through Employee Engagement*. Washington, D.C. www.executiveboard.com

Cotter, John J. 1995. *The 20% Solution: Using Rapid Redesign to Recreate Tomorrow's Organizations Today*. John Wiley & Sons

Covey, Stephen R. 1989. *The 7 Habits of Highly Effective People*. New York: Simon & Shuster.

Covey, Stephen R. 2005. *The 8th Habit: From Effectiveness to Greatness*. New York: Free Press.

Christofferson, Jean; King, Robert E. 2006. "The 'It' Factor: A New Total Rewards Model Leads the Way." *workspan*, April, 19 – 27.

Deal, Terence E.; Key, M.K. 1998. *Corporate Celebration: Play, Purpose and Profit at Work*. San Francisco: Berrett-Koehler.

Deming, W. Edwards. 1993. *The New Economics for Industry, Government, Education*. Cambridge: MIT Press. Cited in the Preface (pg. xi) of Corporate Celebration by Deal and Key.

Doskoch, Peter. 1996. "Happily Ever Laughter." *Psychology Today*, July/August. New York: Sussex Publishers, LLC.

Gallozzi, Chuck. No date. "Benefits of Laughter." www.personal-development.com

Hundley, Stephen P.; Jacobs, Frederic; Drizin, Marc. 2007. *Workforce Engagement: Strategies to Attract, Motivate & Retain Talent*. Scottsdale: WorldatWork Press.

Kaye, Beverly; Jordan-Evans, Sharon. 2005. *Love 'em or lose 'em*. San Francisco: Berrett-Koehler.

Loehr, Jim; Schwartz, Tony. 2003. *The Power of Full Engagement*. New York: Free Press.

Lundin, Stephen C. 2000. *FISH! - A Remarkable Way to Boost Morale and Improve Results*. New York: Hyperion.

Lundin, Stephen C. et al. 2002. *Fish! Tales*. New York: Hyperion.

Miller, John G. 1998. *Personal Accountability*. Brighton: Denver Press.

Miller, John G. 2004. *QBQ! The Question Behind the Question*. New York: Putnam.

Pagano, Barbara; Pagano, Elizabeth. 2003. *Transparency Edge: How Credibility Can Make or Break You in Business*. New York: McGraw-Hill.

Peters, Tom. 2003. *Re-imagine! Business Excellence in a Disruptive Age*. London: Dorling Kindersley Limited.

Rath, Tom; Clifton, Donald O. 2004. *How Full is Your Bucket: Positive Strategies for Work and Life*. Omaha: Gallup Press.

Ruiz, don Miguel. 1997. *The Four Agreements*. San Rafael: Amber-Allen.

Ruiz, don Miguel. 2000. *The Four Agreements Companion Book*. San Rafael: Amber-Allen.

Ruiz, Gina. "Shaking up the Toy Shop." *Workforce Management*, June 26, 2006. (p 26- 34).

Scott, Susan. 2004. *Fierce Conversations: Achieving Success at Work and in Life One Conversation at a Time*. New York: Berkley Trade.

Shafer, Paul; Fischetti, Virginia. 2005. "Rewarding Your Way To Double-Digit Growth." *WorldatWork Journal*, Fourth Quarter, 6 – 15.

Taub, Edward. 1999. *Balance your Body, Balance Your Life*. New York: Kensington Publishing Corporation.

Tracy, Brian. 2002. *The Psychology of Achievement: Develop the Top Achiever's Mindset* (audio CD).

Ulrich, Dave; Smallwood, Norm. 2006. "Leaders Matter." *Link & Learn e-newsletter.* http://www.linkageinc.com, March.

Walsh, James J. 1928. *Laughter and Health.* D. Appleton & Company.

Wellins, Richard S.; Bernthal, Paul; Phelps, Mark, 2001. "Employee Engagement: *The Key to Realizing Competitive Advantage.*" Pittsburgh: Development Dimensions International.

Wooten, R.N., Patty. 1996. *Compassionate Laughter: Jest for Your Health.* Salt Lake City, Utah: Commune-a-Key Publishing.

Zander, Rosamund Stone; Zander, Benjamin. 2000. *The Art of Possibility: Transforming Professional and Personal Life.* Boston: Harvard Business School Press.

Selected References

WorldatWork Articles

Armitage, Amelia. 2004. "Overcoming the 'Elephant Problem': Creating Value with Corporate Performance Management Through Strategic Alignment and Engagement." *WorldatWork Journal*, Third Quarter, 35 – 45.

Banka, Carri. 2002. "Lessons in Best Practices: The Evolution of Performance Management." *workspan*, July, 53 - 54.

Baumruk, Ray. 2004. "The Missing Link: The Role of Employee Engagement in Business Success." *workspan*, November, 49 – 52.

Belliveau, Paul L. 2004. "Feeding the Sandwich Generation." *WorldatWork Journal*, Fourth Quarter, 25 – 31.

Blackburn, Jan; Bremen, John M. 2003. "From Exporting to Integrating: Optimizing Total Rewards for a Global Sales Force." *WorldatWork Journal*, Fourth Quarter, 72 – 79.

Bond, James T.; Galinsky, Ellen; Hill, E. Jeffrey. 2005. "Flexibility: A Critical Ingredient in Creating an Effective Workplace." *workspan*, February, 17 - 22.

Cafaro, Dan. 2003. "No More Blue Mondays." *workspan*, June, 48 - 51.

Chou, Kerry; Risher, Howard. 2005. "Pay for Performance: Point – Counterpoint." *workspan*, September, 28 - 37.

Drizin, Marc. 2005. "Let's Get Engaged: Benchmarks Help Employers Drive Results." *workspan*, April, 47 – 49.

Ellis, Christian M. 2002. "Improving the Impact of Performance Management." *workspan*, February, 7 - 8.

Ferracone, Robin A. 2004. "Break from the Herd: Meeting the Long-term Performance Challenge." *WorldatWork Journal*, Second Quarter, 45 – 55.

Finesod, Rosalyn; Davenport, Thomas O. 2006. "The Aging Workforce: Challenge or Opportunity?" *WorldatWork Journal*, Third Quarter, 14 – 23.

Fineman, Michal. 2004. "Get the Most out of Assessing Your Work Environment." *workspan*, May, 42 - 46.

Gagen, Kathy. 2002. "One Day at a Time: Using Performance Management to Translate Strategy into Results." *workspan*, February, 20 - 25.

Gebauer, Julie; O'Neal, Sandra. 2006. "Talent Management in the 21st Century: Attracting, Retaining and Engaging Employees of Choice." *WorldatWork Journal*, First Quarter, 6 – 17.

Giancola, Frank. 2005. "A Total Rewards Design Tool that Measures Up." *WorldatWork Journal*, Third Quarter, 5 – 12.

Gostick, Adrian. 2003. "A Hero's Welcome: Improving Culture with Noncash Rewards and Recognition." *workspan*, July, 44 - 47.

Greenberg, Richard. 2004. "Beyond Performance Management: Four Principles of Leadership." *workspan*, September, 41 - 45.

Graham, Michael. 2005. "The Rewards of Total Rewards." *workspan*, November, 31 – 35.

Heneman, Robert L.; LeBlanc, Peter V.; Reynolds, Tim L. 2002. "Using Work Valuation to Identify and Protect the Talent Pool." *WorldatWork Journal*, Third Quarter, 32 - 41.

Jesuthasan, Ravin. 2003. "Business Performance Management: Improving Return on Rewards Investments." *WorldatWork Journal*, Fourth Quarter, 55 - 64.

Jones, Keith D. 2005. "The Culture Quandary: Creating An Organizational Fit." *workspan*, October, 12 – 13.

Kadilak, Kathryn O.; Watts, Diana. 2006. "Revisiting the Work-Life Dialogue." *workspan*, May, 38 – 42.

Kantor, Richard; Kao, Tina. 2004. "Total Rewards: Clarity from the Confusion and Chaos." *WorldatWork Journal*, Third Quarter, 6 – 15.

Kao, Tina; Kantor, Richard. 2004. "Total Rewards: From Clarity to Action." *WorldatWork Journal*, Fourth Quarter, 31 – 40.

Lawler, Edward E; McDermott, Michael. 2003. "Current Performance Management Practices: Examining the Varying Impacts." *WorldatWork Journal*, Second Quarter, 49 – 60.

Levine, Brian; Nugent, Kim. 2005. "Rethinking Careers to Enhance Business Performance." *WorldatWork Journal*, Third Quarter, 56 – 63.

Lingle, Kathleen M. 2005. "Employer of Choice is in the Eye of the Beholder." *WorldatWork Journal*, Third Quarter, 26 – 31.

Masuda, Bertha; Barens, Kristin. 2004. "Innovative Trends in Private Companies." *workspan*, September, 23 – 30.

Meyer, Kathryn. 2005. "Survival of the Fittest: Creating a Committed and Engaged Workforce." *workspan*, May, 47 – 51.

Merriman, Kimberly. 2005. "Avoiding the Performance Pay Employee Entitlement Trap." *workspan*, May, 63 – 68.

Mitchell, Kenneth. 2006. "Creating New Horizons: Productive Aging as a Corporate Strategy." *WorldatWork Journal*, Third Quarter, 6 – 13.

Muha, Beth; Mitchell, Carol Vallone; Schaffer, Patricia; Pettit, John. 2003. "Cultural Change, the American University Way." *workspan*, October, 44 – 47.

O'Neal, Sandra. 2005. "Total Rewards and the Future of Work." *workspan*, January, 18 - 26

Ozias, Andrea. 2003. "Exploring the Role of Performance Management." *workspan*, June, 52 – 55.

Parus, Barbara. 2004. "Pump Up Your Flexibility Quotient." *workspan*, August, 47 – 53.

Parus, Barbara. 2003. "The Show Must Go On: Talent Management Sets the Stage for Business Success." *workspan*, July, 48 – 51.

Parus, Barbara. 2003. "Workplace Stress: How Do Employees Get Relief?" *workspan*, June, 40-43.

Parus, Barbara. 2002. "Effective Rewards Support Culture Change." *workspan*, November, 20 -23.

Petruniak, Jane; Saulnier, Peter. 2003. "The Total Rewards Sweet Spot." *workspan*, August, 38 – 41.

Piktialis, Diane. 2006. "The Generational Divide in Talent Management." *workspan*, March, 10 – 12.

Polak, Richard. 2006. "Culture in a Box: The Ten Steps of a Successful Company." *workspan*, February, 8 – 9.

Richman, Amy. 2006. "Everyone Wants An Engaged Workforce – How Can You Create It?" *workspan*, January, 36 – 39.

Rodriguez, Eleana. 2002. "Achieving Outstanding Performance Through a Culture of Dialogue." *workspan*, September, 24 – 28.

Rogers, Phil. 2006. "Incentives Can Drive Success in Workplace Wellness Programs." *workspan*, February, 55 – 56.

Satterfield, Terry. 2003. "From Performance Management to Performance Leadership: A Model for Change." *WorldatWork Journal*, First Quarter, 15 – 20.

Schinnerer, John. 2003. "The ROI of an Effective Ethics Program." *workspan*, October, 52 - 55.

Sejen, Laura. 2006. "Total Rewards: 10 Steps to a More Effective Program." *workspan*, April, 36 – 39.

Starzmann, Gary; Baca, Carrie. 2004. "Total Rewards: Creating Freshness That Lasts." *workspan*, October, 69 – 72.

Stoskopf, Gregory. 2004. "Using Total Rewards to Attract and Retain Health Care Employees." *WorldatWork Journal*, Third Quarter, 15 – 25.

Sung, Amy; Todd, Emory. 2004. "Line of Sight: Moving Beyond the Catchphrase." *workspan*, October, 44- 49.

Watson, Stephen. 2003. "Total Rewards: Building a Better Employment Deal." *workspan*, December, 48 – 51.

WorldatWork Surveys (www.worldatwork.org/library/research/ surveys)

Aligning Rewards with the Changing Employment Deal – 2006/2007 Strategic Rewards Report

Flexible Work Schedules Survey Brief – 2005

Trends in Employee Recognition Survey Brief – 2005

The State of Performance Management Survey Brief - 2004

WorldatWork Bookstore (www.worldatwork.org/bookstore)

Barton, G. Michael. 2002. *Recognition at Work*. Scottsdale: WorldatWork Press.

Bellingham, Richard. 2001. *The Manager's Pocket Guide to Corporate Culture Change.* Amherst: HRD Press. St. Louis: Elsevier Butterworth-Heinemann.

Carsen, Jennifer A. 2003. *HR How-to: Employee Retention: Everything You Need To Know About Creating an Effective Employee Retention Program.* Riverwoods: Petaluma: CCH Knowledge Point.

Conner, Daryl R. 2006. *Managing the Speed of Change: How Resilient Managers Succeed and Prosper Where Others Fail.* New York: Random House.

Dauten, Dale. 2006. *Better than Perfect: How Gifted Bosses and Great Employees Can Lift the Performance of Those Around Them.* Franklin Lakes: Career Press.

Dundon, Elaine. 2002. *The Seeds of Innovation: Cultivating the Synergy That Fosters New Ideas.* New York: AMACOM.

Dychtwald, Ken; Erickson, Tamara J.; Morison, Robert. 2006. *Workforce Crisis: How to Beat the Coming Shortage of Skills and Talents.* Boston: Harvard Business School Press.

Flaherty, James. 2005. *Coaching: Evoking Excellence In Others.* Atlanta: Elsevier.

Gallagher, Richard S. 2003. *The Soul of an Organization: Understanding the Values that Drive Successful Corporate Cultures.* Chicago: Dearborn Trade Publishing.

Gandossy, Robert P.; Tucker, Elissa; Verma, Nidhi. 2006. Workforce Wake-Up Call: *Your Workforce Is Changing, Are You?* San Francisco: John Wiley & Sons.

Harris, Philip R.; Moran, Robert T.; Moran, Sarah V. 2004. *Managing Cultural Difference: Global Leadership Strategies for the Twenty-first Century.* St. Louis: Elsevier Butterworth-Heinemann.

Holbeche, Linda. 2005. *The High Performance Organization: Creating Dynamic Stability and Sustainable Success.* Engelwood: Elsevier Butterworth-Heinemann.

Holtz, Shel. 2004. *Corporate Conversations: A Guide to Crafting Effective And Appropriate Internal Communications.* New York: AMACOM.

Horibe, Frances. 2001. *Creating the Innovation Culture: Leveraging Visionaries, Dissenters and Other Useful Troublemakers in Your Organization.* San Francisco: John Wiley & Sons.

Kaye, Beverly; Jordan-Evans, Sharon. 2005. Love *'Em or Lose 'Em: Getting Good People to Stay,* 3d, San Francisco: Berrett-Koehler.

Kirkpatrick, Donald L. 2006. *Improving Employee Performance Through Appraisal and Coaching.* New York: AMACOM.

Lawler, Edward III. 2003. Treat People Right: *How Organizations and Individuals Can Propel Each Other Into a Virtuous Spiral of Success.* San Francisco: Jossey-Bass.

Ledford, Gerald E. 2003. *The 2003 Rewards of Work: The Employment Deal in a Changing Economy.* New York: Sibson Consulting.

Markowich, Michael M. 2006. *Paid Time Off Banks: Program Design and Implementation.* Scottsdale: WorldatWork.

O'Toole, James; Lawler III, Edward E. 2006. *The New American Workplace.* New York: Palgrave MacMillan.

Phillips, Jack J. 2003. *Managing Employee Retention: A Strategic Accountability Approach.* Englewood: Butterworth-Heinemann.

Phillips, Jack J. 2002. *Retaining Your Best Employees: Nine Case Studies from the Real World of Training.* Alexandria: SHRM.

Porter, Keith; Smith, Paul; Fagg, Roger. 2004. *Leadership and Management for HR Professionals.* St. Louis: Butterworth-Heinemann.

Rogers, Susan; Lohwater, Karl W.; Hager, Holly. 2006. Communicating Total Rewards: *How-to Series for the HR Professional.* Scottsdale: WorldatWork.

Rose, Karol. 2006. Work-Life Effectiveness: *Bottom-Line Strategies for Today's Workplace.* Scottsdale: WorldatWork.

Rosen, Corey; Carberry, Ed. 2002. *Ownership Management: Building a Culture of Lasting Innovation.* Oakland: National Center for Employee Ownership.

Senge, Peter; Scharmer, Otto: Jaworski, Joseph; Flowers, Betty Sue. 2005. *Presence: An Exploration of Profound Change in People, Organizations, and Society.* Cambridge: Society for Organizational Learning.

WorldatWork. 2005. Cash Bonuses: *Four Ways to Attract, Retain and Motivate Employees,* 2d. Scottsdale: WorldatWork.

WorldatWork. 2002. *Best of Attraction and Retention.* Scottsdale: WorldatWork.

WorldatWork. 2003. *Best of Performance Management: A Collection of Articles from WorldatWork.* Scottsdale: WorldatWork Press.

Zachary, Lois J. 2005. *Creating a Mentoring Culture.* Hoboken: Jossey-Bass.

Zingheim, Patricia K; Schuster, Jay R. 2000. *Pay People Right! Breakthrough Reward Strategies to Create Great Companies.* San Francisco: Jossey-Bass.

WorldatWork Courses (www.worldatwork.org/education)

T1: Total Rewards Management

T4: Strategic Communication in Total Rewards

C11: Performance Management – Strategy, Design and Implementation

W1: Introduction to Work-Life Effectiveness —
Successful Work-Life Programs to Attract, Motivate and Retain Employees
Understand the Impact of Work-Life Effectiveness

W2: The Flexible Workplace — Strategies for Your Organization
Heighten Employee and Organizational Effectiveness

W3: Health and Wellness Programs — Creating a Positive Business Impact
Incorporate Health and Wellness into Your Organization

About the Author

Sandy Asch, principal of Alliance for Organizational Excellence LLC, leads a consortium of management and organizational development consultants with more than 18 years of success helping companies meet the challenges of today's competitive workplace.

Asch and her team specialize in working with managers and leaders to build workplace excellence and gain the reputation as an employer of choice so they can attract, optimize and retain top talent to meet and exceed their company's goals. Asch has worked with a variety of organizations in the high-tech, biotech, telecom, financial services, consumer products, manufacturing, and defense industries. More than 10,000 individuals from 300-plus companies have participated in her programs as a means to achieve improved results, including Pepsi, Qualcomm Inc., General Atomics-ASI, Biosite, E&J Gallo Wineries, International Paper, Universal City, Hollywood, Metabolife, DR Horton Homebuilders, and Modern Postcard.

She is a frequent presenter to human resources groups and an approved speaker for Vistage International, where she presents to executive groups internationally on how to become a sustainable employer of choice. Asch is co-author of *The Complete 360-Degree Feedback Resource Kit*, a comprehensive best practices guide for the HR/OD/Training Professional to design, prepare, train and debrief the organization for the 360-degree feedback process.

A member of the San Diego Society for Human Resource Management, North County Personnel Association, American Society for Training and Development and the Organizational Development Network, Asch holds a master's degree in organizational management and has taught graduate and undergraduate classes in management, organizational behavior and human resources management.

She can be reached at sandy@Uexcel.com or by phone at 858/481-7742. Her Web site is www.Uexcel.com.